The Aventures of Alys
in Wondyr Lond

The Aventures
of Alys
in Wondyr Lond

by Lewis Carroll

WITH ILLUSTRATIONS BY
BYRON W. SEWELL

TRANSLATED INTO MIDDLE ENGLISH VERSE
BY BRIAN S. LEE

evertype

2013

Published by Evertype, Cnoc Sceichín, Leac an Anfa, Cathair na Mart, Co. Mhaigh Eo, Éire. *www.evertype.com*.

Original title: *Alice's Adventures in Wonderland*.

First edition 2013.

ISBN-10 1-78201-031-9
ISBN-13 978-1-78201-031-9

Typeset in De Vinne Text, Mona Lisa, ENGRAVERS' ROMAN, *Liberty*, and 𝔘𝔫𝔤 𝔅𝔞𝔰𝔱𝔞𝔯𝔡𝔢 Manual Normal by Michael Everson.

Illustrations: Byron W. Sewell. Illustrations on pages 72 and 103 by John Tenniel, 1865.

Cover: Michael Everson.

Printed by LightningSource.

Introduction

Why translate *Alice's Adventures in Wonderland* into an obsolete form of English? We may think medieval people unfortunate not to have had the chance to enjoy Lewis Carroll's wise and witty parody of the life and language of his Victorian contemporaries, but it seems too late to help them now. Perhaps, though, the translation suggests sympathy with Carroll's rebellion, symbolized by the Hatter's well-buttered pocket watch, against the tyranny of relentlessly forward marching time. Technologically the Victorians had mastered Time, as the formidably accurate new clock, dating from 1859, on the Houses of Parliament suggested, but thereby they had shackled themselves to a seemingly unnatural demand for punctuality, and a frightening awareness of the rapid passing of life. It is surprising how often death is mentioned in the book: from the Mouse's tale to the Queen's croquet game and the Knave's trial it is always threatening to curtail proceedings, but never actually does.

Middle English is the name commonly given to the forms of English current from about 1100 to roughly 1500, between pre-Conquest Old English, which is hardly intelligible today without special study, and the early modern English of Shakespeare and his contemporaries. Of course it changed considerably during that period, and different dialects existed in various geographical areas. Those to the east of a line more or less stretching from Chester to the Wash, East Midland and Northern as far as the border with Scotland, which were affected by Viking incursions and settlement, gave rise to our standard Modern English and so are easier to read now than West Midland which did not.

The form of Middle English that I have chosen to imitate is for the most part the East Midland and London dialect of writers like Chaucer in the fourteenth century, which is the direct ancestor of our modern standard form of English.

> *Ye knowe ek that in forme of speche is chaunge*
> *Withinne a thousand yeer, and wordes tho*
> *That hadden pris, now wonder nyce and straunge*
> *Us thinketh hem, and yet thei spake hem so ...*
>
> (*Troilus* II, 22-25)

Thus Chaucer reminds us of the inevitability of linguistic change, and incidentally illustrates its nature: in this passage from *Troilus and Criseyde*, most of the words are familiar, if slightly oddly spelt; some like *tho*, contrasting with *now*, can easily be guessed from the context to mean 'then'; *pris*, 'price' or 'prize', will mean 'value' or more specifically in the context 'currency'; *ek* meaning 'also' is possibly the only word in the passage that may be unfamiliar, but *nyce* in the sense of 'quaint' or 'foolish' might easily be misunderstood. The grammar too is familiar, except *Us thinketh* for 'we think', where *thinketh* is actually an impersonal verb meaning 'seems', the phrase literally meaning 'it seems to us'.

There is a plural imperative (not in this passage), also ending -(*e*)*th*, used when addressing more than one person, and also on occasion as a mark of respect when addressing a single person: *Goth to your stedes!* 'Go to your places!' *Redeth, Heraud* 'Herald, read!'

Much later in his poem (V, 1796) Chaucer prays *"that non myswrite the, / Ne the mysmetre for defaute of tonge"*—that no-one, that is, no scribe or reader trying to assimilate Chaucer's English to his own dialect, might copy you wrongly or mis-metre you (that is, the poem, and spoil its metre) because of deficiency of dialect, or lack of knowledge of Chaucer's London English. Here *the* would today be spelt "thee", a doubled vowel being merely an indication of length, not of a change of vowel quality. *Myswrite* shows that *i* and *y* medially or finally were interchangeable, and that the metre requires that the final *e* (a neutral vowel like the *a* in "China") be pronounced, as it always is if the syllable count requires it. In the passage quoted from Book II most of the final *e*'s elide before a following vowel, even in *spake* (where the *a* will not be a diphthong as today, but pronounced like the a in "back") before the ignored *h* of *hem*; but the final syllables of *wordes* and *hadden* are pronounced, as the iambic pentameter metre requires. The subject plural form 'they' is here spelt *thei*, but the object form 'them' and the possessive 'their' in Middle English are always *hem* and *hir*.

Such are some of the linguistic changes that must be observed when translating *Alice's Adventures in Wonderland*. The translation offered here is in verse, because, until the advent of the long prose romances, a medieval *proces* or narrative usually was in verse, for ease of recitation, prose being reserved for treatises or what would nowadays be called non-fiction. A verse narrative would be intended, though not exclusively, for hearers and for reading aloud, and so it is important to get the pronunciation right. Words that look odd will often become clear when spoken or imagined aloud. Simple rules to remember are that single or doubled vowels are always either long or short and not diphthongized, *e* when not the neutral vowel being pronounced as in French rather than English, so that *me* or *thee* does not rhyme with *whi*, *(e)ye* or *-ly*; that diphthongs spelt *ai*, *ay*, *ei*, or *ey* are all pronounced [aɪ] as *ai* in "aisle" or *i* in "shine"; that *ou* and *ow* are pronounced [u:] as *u* in "true" or *ou* in "you"; and that consonants now silent are to be sounded, as the *k* in *knee* or the *gh* in *right*. Thus in Middle English *knyght*, all the consonants will be pronounced, the *gh* a velar fricative like the *ch* in Scottish "loch", and the *y* as the *i* in "tin": [knɪxt].

In what follows rhymes may be assumed to be exact despite spelling differences, though admittedly sometimes insufficient notice may be taken of long and short vowels. Middle English also accepted, as rhyming, words of identical sound, provided their meaning was different, e.g. *welle* (adverb) and *welle* (the noun). Though the dialect preferred is that of fourteenth- century London, some words that might have belonged to other dialects of English or even seemed obsolete to Chaucer, Langland or Gower have as occasion demanded been admitted. Middle Scots was readily distinguished from Middle English, so the White Rabbit's Irish servant Pat almost inevitably becomes Andrew from Scotland. Communications in medieval England being less swift than they are today, dialectal differences were many and for the most part not hierarchical: London English, because of the capital's political importance, was only just beginning to acquire the prestige that was later to make it standard. The Cockney class-dialect of such characters as the Gryphon, for example, was not yet the social marker it had become in Carroll's day and will therefore be less obvious in the translation than in the original.

Alice's Adventures already has a medieval twist, albeit via Shakespeare, in that Lewis Carroll doubtless borrowed the Queen's favourite cry "Off with his head!" from that "tiger's heart wrapped in a woman's hide" Queen Margaret (*III Henry VI*, Act I, Scene 4), whose meek husband was the fifteenth-century monarch Henry VI; it was she who in *II Henry VI*, Act I Scene 3 dropped her fan and boxed the Duchess's ears for not picking it up. Alice's dream, which projects a new world that reflects upon the old, in this respect has affinities with the dream visions of Langland and Chaucer, and its protagonist embarks upon a voyage of self-discovery, as do theirs, as she encounters the wonders with which she is confronted.

Alice finds herself in a world that is a parody of the one she is familiar with, where even physical laws may not apply, where the rules of social contact differ, and where persons or creatures think associatively instead of logically. She responds as modern people encountering the Middle Ages for the first time often do: with amusement or contempt, sometimes even hostility, until she grows more respectful as she learns to understand it better.

A work like *Alice's Adventures in Wonderland*, which is all about change, invites the change that translation implies. As might be expected of a mathematician, Carroll measures Alice's various sizes with some precision, to accord with the real size of the little creatures she interacts with, or frightens when too large, or fears if too small. If logic sometimes demands that they change too, the fact may be overlooked in a fantasy: the pig and flamingoes Alice carries when she is nine inches high must be abnormally small, and since she has to grow to a height of two feet in order to take tea with the Hatter, he ought to be too large to be so afraid of the King and Queen of Hearts, unless he and his friends had mysteriously shrunk between teatable and courtroom. But in a dream it is only the protagonist's experiences, those of the dreamer herself, that are significant. When the Cheshire Cat disappears Alice wonders not as we might where it has gone but only that its remarkable grin should outlast the rest of it. Sudden growth affects even her grammar: "Curiouser and curiouser!" she famously remarks as she shoots up to over nine feet high. Carroll is wryly amused at the pedantry of Victorian school-teachers, who in their zeal for "correctness" would regard such mild solecisms as "bad" English. Alice's changes in stature are important as physical manifestations of the subtler changes in language, outlook and behaviour that Lewis Carroll's imagination portrays.

The story is a fantasy, that is, an answer to the question "What might things be like if, impossibly, they were different?" The Queen's executions are all her fantasy; so is the Mock Turtle's sorrow, as the Gryphon explains. But literal-minded Alice, although living her own fantasy in Wonderland, rejects as implausible the Dormouse's fantasy of a treacle well. The idea of drawing sweet-tasting treacle from a well might delight an imaginative Victorian child, but practical Alice thinks only of the cloying consequences of over-indulgence. Ironically, *triacle* in the Middle Ages meant an antidote to poison, a panacea for physical ailments, so the medieval "Dormous", unlike its Victorian counterpart, makes the point that the three little girls (Alys and her two sisters?)[1] in the *triacle* well are not sick but in radiant health! Fictionally, the entire dream is a fantasy that takes place in Alice's head; actually, in Lewis Carroll's, whose name is itself a fantasy. Carroll is like the Cheshire Cat with its ubiquitous enigmatic grin, appearing and disappearing unexpectedly; Alice sees it in a tree suggested by the horse chestnut in the

---

1 Alluding to the Liddell girls, Carroll names the sisters in the well Elsie (L.C. for Lorina Charlotte), Lacie (anagram of Alice) and Tillie, (short for Matilda, Edith's nickname). I have changed the names to commoner medieval ones, but punned later on Alice's middle name, Pleasance (line 1754).

Dean's garden at Christ Church College in Oxford, where Charles Dodgson watched Alice Liddell playing.

The Cheshire Cat has materialized out of a phrase. "To grin like a Cheshire Cat," whatever the origin of the simile, is recorded in the eighteenth century, long before Lewis Carroll popularized it. The March Hare is mad because people are wont to say "As mad as a March Hare." Mock turtle soup[2] implies the existence of a Mock Turtle, who believes he was once a real turtle, though he does not tell us how he became an imitation. Alice has problems understanding characters who are metaphors made literal: their frame of reference differs from the way she has been brought up to see the world. Language and events follow a logic of their own: calling a baby "Pig!" is enough to change it into one; if Alice's watch has no need to record the year since it stays so long unchanged, the Hatter's need not indicate the hour, since for him it is always the tea-hour.

Puns, one might say, are the lynch-pins of *Alice's Adventures*, suggesting not so much the distinction between fantasy and reality as their merging. Disparate objects are associated because of a fancied likeness of sound in the words that refer to them, not because of what in fact they are. That puns do not always work in translation indicates their arbitrary or fantastic nature. "Tortoise" and "taught us" sound the same in Victorian English; *tortus* and *taught us* do not in Middle English, so something else has to be found. For a different reason, that of anachronism, the pun on "T" and "tea" is not available in a Middle English translation. Only words already part of the language before the sixteenth century can be admitted: dodos were known, though extinct, in Lewis Carroll's time, but not even known in medieval

---

2. Mock turtle soup was made from veal and pork, hence the illustrations show the Mock Turtle with a calf's head and tail, and pigs' trotters.

England; so the fantastic Dodo is replaced by the fabulous Phoenix, to which the Middle Ages knew classical references, and regarded them as more important than its probable non-existence.

Figurative expressions common enough today, like "a bright idea came into Alice's head", or "his eye chanced to fall upon Alice" might have raised medieval eyebrows, and have had to be avoided. The latter has been replaced by a tautology that is attested from the Middle Ages (line 1804).

In the world that Alice enters, or rather invades, puns denote reality to the creatures who use them: the Mock Turtle (himself a pun) and the Gryphon are angry at and contemptuous of Alice's failure to realize this. If it is possible in speech to speak to time, or to beat time, then in Wonderland it may be done literally. Accordingly the Hatter regards Time as a person capable of ill-treatment, to Alice's bewilderment, and his entire lifestyle is affected; she leaves the tea-table in disgust, but the only change available to him, who in singing murdered the time, is to move from one place setting to the next. Even at the trial he has to continue his never-ending tea-party, where his mental confusion is such that it is perhaps not surprising that he is frightened into biting a piece out of his teacup instead of from his bread and butter.

The logic thus defied and the Hatter's non sequiturs that so puzzle Alice have their effect most noticeably in the ridiculously chaotic trial scene, from which only injustice can result. It is the witness with no evidence to give whose life is in danger, rather than the defendant's, whose guilt is never established or disproved. "Sentence first—verdict afterwards" is an inversion quite consistent with the Queen's character, but thoroughly unacceptable to Alice. That Carroll is casting doubt on the complacent certainties of Victorian culture is clear; how far a translation into medieval circumstances will bring out similarities of unconscionable medieval behaviour will depend probably on a reader's knowledge of history.

Alice's "Adventures in Wonderland" might have been entitled her "Invasion of Wonderland" for anyone wishing to read the fantasy as a critique of Victorian imperial expansionism and colonization. In the alien environment in which she finds herself Alice gets into an argument with almost the first creature she meets, the Lory (an exotic species of parrot, and therefore *Papengaye*), and shows a callous inability to appreciate the dismay her praise of the cat she loves will cause to the creatures such an animal preys upon, even after the Mouse has clearly explained why he hates cats. Alice is too busy puzzling over the pun on *tail* and *tale* (which fortunately also works in Middle English) to listen properly. It rarely seems to have occurred to the imperialists that the natives whom they sought to civilize, or destroyed when they objected, might have a right to their own apparently inferior life style. Of a similar nature were the forcible conversions of pagans or Saracens for which the Middle Ages are notorious.

Alice takes over—completely!—the White Rabbit's bedroom, and forcibly ejects the servant who tries to get in and clear it. Like an over-enthusiastic social worker, she insists on entering the Duchess's house, though the Frog footman sees no reason to admit her, voices her disapproval of what she finds inside, and kidnaps the baby lest its home circumstances should, as she thinks likely, kill it. She calls those she cannot understand, notably the Hatter and March Hare, rude, but is soon convicted of even greater rudeness herself; it is only after she has managed to get into the beautiful garden that she begins to show respect for those she meets there. Failure to appreciate aliens was hardly more marked in the Middle Ages: Chaucer's *Man of Law's Tale* shows trading and even intermarriage with Saracens, though the outcome is murder and mayhem. Historically, the King of Tharsis, seeking relief from the plague that was decimating his people, led a multitude to the Pope in Avignon to be converted—he would hardly have fared better had he chosen the other Pope in Rome—but finding that the plague had crossed the Alps ahead of him, decided the expedition was pointless and turned homewards, whereupon the Christians, so-called, fell upon the retreating host and slaughtered two thousand of them. No one dies, of course, in *Alice's Adventures,* but the threat is certainly there, from the judicial condemning to death in the tale the Mouse tells to the way all the guests at the Queen's croquet party end up in prison awaiting execution. Instead of apologetically seeking assistance when trapped in the White Rabbit's house, Alice responds with violence and threats to the Rabbit's legitimate attempts to free his house of its invader.

Alice's generally superior or hostile attitude changes as she learns to take control of her changes in stature, which she does by conscious manipulation of the Caterpillar's mushroom, instead of simply trusting to whatever magic may be in the drinks or cakes she finds to swallow. Her interview with the Caterpillar highlights her awareness of change as a matter of identity. For the Caterpillar changing into a butterfly holds no qualms, but for Alice the question "Who are you?" is one she is no longer sure how to answer. It is a psychological problem becoming increasingly relevant in Lewis Carroll's rapidly evolving Victorian society, but not one that seems to have much troubled medieval people, for whom the question rather was "Whose side are you on?"— God's or the Devil's? Do you acknowledge the Pope (though which one, in the schismatic fourteenth century, was an issue) or Mohammed? Are you Jew or Christian? Is your King that of England, or one of the Continental monarchs? Chaucer's characters in *The Canterbury Tales* are as much types as individuals. In the chapter where Alice meets the

Caterpillar and the Pigeon, her size and indeed form are at
their most extreme: either she is three inches tall, or
shrinking so rapidly that her chin strikes her foot (and
presumably almost knocks her out!) or so elongated that her
neck towering above the treetops resembles a serpent's. Is
she a girl or a serpent?—both, after all, eat eggs.

Her snobbish class-consciousness is inadvertently revealed
as she bemoans the possibility that she may have changed
into the disadvantaged Mabel, who besides being foolish lives
in a poor cottage, like the Widow in the *Nun's Priest's Tale,*
and has hardly any toys to play with but an awful lot of
catching up on schoolwork to do. At home Alice has a nurse
to tell her when to get ready for her walk and presumably
supervise her meals; in Wonderland she is on her own, and
takes advantage of her freedom. She sits down uninvited at
the March Hare's tea-table, where there seems to be plenty
of room, and helps herself, because she does not realize it is
his table, for so much of it is unoccupied. Like the little maid
who is *under yerde* ('discipline') in *The Shipman's Tale,* she
enjoys constant supervision in real life, and accordingly the
Mock Turtle imagines the Gryphon has some sort of
authority over her. Even in Wonderland when required to,
she has no option but to repeat her lessons, however faulty
her performance, and however much she balks at being
ordered about by the creatures she finds there.

The world of Wonderland is Victorian reality skewed.
Hence the poems taught to children by Victorian teachers
become parodies of their originals. In a Middle English
version the change in the direction of medieval literary forms
makes them parodies either of themselves or else where it
seemed appropriate of well-known medieval texts. Thus I
have replaced Carroll's parody of Jane Taylor's *"Twinkle"*
poem with a parody of the lilting refrain of the early
fourteenth-century love lyric "Alysoun". While Carroll

startles us with his delightfully apt but grotesque "tea-tray", I have introduced a falling tile, and rhymed "croun" with the "Alysoun" of the original (line 1624b).

Alice's education is a constant theme of her adventures. She is proud to display her knowledge, whether of geography while falling towards the centre or other side of the earth, or of astronomy when telling the Duchess how long it takes the earth to spin. In the Middle Ages the only known and supposedly knowable continent was on one side of the Northern hemisphere of the world, Taprobana (Ceylon) being both farthest South-east and on medieval *mappae-mundi* (world maps, or rather diagrams of the way the divinely ordained cosmos was understood) opposite the British Isles in the far North-west, so there, rather than in the as yet undiscovered New Zealand, is where Alice expects to land. The planets were supposed to revolve on concentric spheres around the central Earth, so it is the Ptolemaic celestial system and not the modern Copernican one that Alice explains to the Duchess.

Carroll parodies not only poems but schoolbooks currently in use. The Mouse's "dry" lesson that fails to dry his soaking wet "pupils" is taken from Haviland Chepmell's *Short Course in History*. Here the quotation appears in "rhyme royal", a stanza form Chaucer uses for his most serious poetry.

Medieval education, after the elementary primer stage, was geared towards the learning of Latin, so that England, where the aristocrats spoke Anglo-French and the majority of the populace English, was tri-lingual. Alice seems to know a little of each. She has learnt from her brother's "donat" (line 405), the *Ars Minor* or "Lesser Catechism in the Parts of Speech" of the fourth-century Roman schoolmaster Aelius Donatus, that the way to address the Mouse in the pool of tears is to say "O Mus". Alice Liddell had an older brother Harry, and Carroll doubtless alludes to whichever Victorian Latin textbook he was required to study, but Carroll may also have had Donatus in mind. Donatus declines nouns in the same order: nominative, genitive, dative, accustive, vocative— that Alice does (line 406), which is not the order commonly used in modern Latin grammars. Naturally, stopping at the vocative since she is about to address the Mouse, Alice omits the sixth case, ablative: there is no need to assume, as has been done, that since classical Greek had no ablative Carroll was alluding to a Greek textbook. Illustrating the declension of nouns grammatically feminine, Donatus includes the phrase "*uocativo o Musa*" ('in the vocative, O Muse'). Alice may have mistakenly thought "Musa" meant "mouse", or else Carroll sees an opportunity for a rather well-hidden pun! Alice, then, to the Mouse's horror, quotes the first sentence of her elementary French grammar (line 419). Continuing with her education in the Middle Ages, she would proceed to the Trivium: Grammar, Rhetoric, and Logic, and then to the Quadrivium: Arithmetic, Music, Geometry, and Astronomy, which were somewhat garbled in Wonderland, as the Mock Turtle's puns indicate.

In a largely oral culture proverbs and mnemonic tags were a staple part of what was taught; the Duchess's morals, however strangely misapplied, are a form of these. "Cato's" *Distichs,* a popular collection of moral sayings, provide Chaucer's Pertelote, and his Second Nun, with advice, one piece of which a medieval version of Alice's Duchess may be allowed to imitate.

At the end of the trial scene Alice grows back to her full height till she seems nearly two miles high to the King and Queen of Hearts; then she wakes and suddenly she is "little Alice" again, the adjective insisted upon several times. The story's final change is the most startling, if not at first sight the most intriguing: it occurs in what here is called the Epilogue, when Alice awakens and the world returns to "normal" in a manner for which some have found it hard to forgive the author. For the dream Alice has when asleep is so much more vivid than her sister's waking dream that it ought to be more "real", not casually dismissed as if it deserved to be cancelled or denied. Yet this is what Chaucer does in his "Retraction" when he repudiates those tales which are not *"writen for oure doctrine"*, even though they include his greatest complete poem, *Troilus,* and *"the tales of Caunterbury, thilke that sownen into synne"*, the ones we are likely to find the most entertaining. If we are reluctant to take his pious ending seriously, perhaps we may not be wrong to question Lewis Carroll's sentimental one.

The little child with her tiny hands and wayward curl who in the far future will be a grown but still child-like woman telling tales of wonder to other little children experiencing the simple joys and sorrows of childhood is a poor substitute for the dominant and self-opinionated personality who does nevertheless learn to appreciate at least some of her shortcomings. The limited vision of her elder sister regards Alice's adventures as "mere" dislocutions of the ordinary sounds and sights of rural England. The surface blandness of the deceptively beautiful ending is palatable if read as Lewis Carroll's pretended disclaimer of the radical critique of Victorian society that his fantastic remodelling has subjected it to. It is perhaps as well that most readers should see no farther than its primary purpose of presenting a child's fairytale. In this it is not dissimilar to Chaucer's mock-heroic treatment of the fable of the cock and the fox in his inimitable *Nun's Priest's Tale.*

The so-called "Middle" Ages were entirely modern to those who lived in them, but at this distance it may not be easy to appreciate what life and mental attitudes were like so long ago. So how should one read a translation into Middle English of *Alice's Adventures in Wonderland?* As the King advised the White Rabbit, about to read out, aloud, from a paper picked up on the court room floor, "Begin at the beginning, ... go on till you come to the end: then stop." And if at first sight there does not appear to be "an atom of meaning in it," closer inspection may reveal some, after all.

Brian S. Lee
Rosebank, Cape Town, South Africa, 2013

With thanks to John Tenniel.

On Illustrating *Alice* in the 14th century

*I*t has been my very great pleasure to work with Byron W. Sewell on a number of Carrollian projects, from his Snarkian extensions to his Alician parodies *Alix's Adventures in Wonderland: Lewis Carroll's Nightmare, Alice's Bad Hair Day in Wonderland,* and *Álopk's Adventures in Goatland.* These are all utterly splendid and I look forward to much more collaboration with Byron.

When *Alice* is transported to a parallel universe, as in Byron's *Alice's Adventures in an Appalachian Wonderland,* or as here in Brian S. Lee's masterful Middle English *Aventures of Alys in Wondyr Lond,* not only has the text to be anachronistic and believable—but the illustrations must serve the text as well.

It occurred to me to share with the reader just how difficult—and how much fun—this exercise actually is. In the frontispiece and elsewhere, the attire of a fourteenth-century King and Queen and other royals cannot be set in the Tudor period of the modern deck of cards. Here, we based our costuming on that of Richard II, who lived at the same time as Chaucer (both died in 1400). Alys' dress is based on the attire of a child who was more or less of the same relative social class as Alice Liddell. When not at court, the White Coninge wears an ordinary merchant's coat and carries an astrolabe rather than a watch. At court, he wears a medieval tabard identical to that which Tenniel drew, though his collar is different and he wears medieval shoes. The trompe he blows has the shape of a period buisine.

Medievalists should note that the Catirpel is not smoking a hookah, but making use of an alembic, a kind of alchemical vessel, used for distilling chemicals. The clothes of Sir Bertilak and Sir Gawain were inspired by the Knight and the Squire in the fifteenth-century Ellesmere manuscript. The liveries of the house-servant Fotman Frogge and the messenger Fotman Fissch were taken from a contemporary drawing.

We have cheated a bit in keeping the Duchess' attire as it was, it having been based by Tenniel on Flemish artist Quentin Matsys' painting *The Ugly Duchess* (1513).

In general the furniture and accoutrements have been medievalized. Of some interest is the medieval comb held by the Lopstere.

While Hearts and Diamonds (or Lozenges) have the same shape in medieval heraldry as they do in modern playing cards, Spades have been replaced by the spearhead of a Pike and Clubs by the Trefoil. The executioner's axe in Chapter VIII resembles those of period executioners (though the sword was more common) as well as the heraldic axe.

It has been a great pleasure working with both Brian S. Lee and Byron W. Sewell preparing the illustrations for this volume. "For what," hir thought, "help is a bok in whiche ne speche ne peinture nis?"

Michael Everson
Westport, 2013

GRETINGES AT CRISTES MESSE

(FROM A FAYERYE TO A CHILD)

Ladye dere, if fayeryes may
Onë whilë lay on syde
Conninge wrenches, elvish play,
Hit shal be at Yulë-tyde.

We have herde the children say—
Gentil children that we love—
Longe ago, on Yulë-day,
Came a message from above.

Ever yet, whan Yule come round,
They minne hem of hit then—
Yet reherse the joyous sound
"Pes on erthe, gode wille to men!"

But sholde hertës childli be
Wher suche hevenyssh gestes abyde;
Unto children, in her gle,
Al the yere is Yulë-tyde!

Thus, foryettyng wrenche and play
Schortë whilë, Ladye dere,
We wolde wissh you, an we may,
Merie Yule-tyde, glad New Yere!

after Lewis Carroll
Cristes messe, 1867.

The Aventures of Alys in Wondyr Lond

CONTENTS

Beth stil and listeth! Ye shal heere a fitt
Reducëd from a book a clerk hath writ
In aftyr Englyssh, how a yongë mayde,
Alys by name, that lessuns conned but sayde
Noon right ne logik coude whan onë daye   5
Slepyng, as Langland dyde, on medow gaye,
In sweven merueillouse hir thought she found,
Doun in a coningere wel under ground,
No lak of wondrous crëaturës ther
Egre to speke to hir, though mad some wer—   10
Yet most my joly whistle fyrst be wet
Lest lakkyng ale none tale of me ye get!
Excepte blest God sholde give me special grace
Expect I nil this proces put in place.

Alle in the gylden aftyr-noon
    At leyser we forth glide;
For bothe oure arës with smal skile
    Bi litel arms are plied
And litel hands in vayne pretend   5
    Oure wandringës to gide.

A, cruele Thre! In suche an houre
    Binethe suche slepi weder
To beg a tale from brethe to waik
    To stir the smalest feder!   10
But what may oon pore voys avayle
    Ageins thre tungs togeder?

Imperial Prima cryth aloude
    Commaund "to now begin hit":
In gentler voys Secunda seith   15
    "I hope for nonsens in hit!"
And Tertia entremeteth tale
    But onys in a minute.

Anon to sodeyn silence brought
    In fantasye they vewe   20
The dreme childe movyng thurgh a land
    Of wondyrs wilde and newe,
Conversyng freend with brid or beest,
    And half bileve hit trewe.

And ever as the storie drou   25
    Fantasies wellë drye
And feintlye strivëd that mat oon
    To lette the matiere lye,
"The rest nexte tyme—" "This *is* nexte tyme!"
    The merie voyces crye.   30

Thus grew the tale of Wondyr Lond:
    Thus slowly, oon by oon,
The straunge aventures forgëd been
    And now the tale is doon,
And ham we stere, a merie crewe,   35
    As ginneth sunne doun goon.

Alys! A childish storie take,
    And with a gentil hand,
Lay hit wher Childheds swevenes twine
    In Memories straunge band,   40
Lyk pilgrims wedered writhe of floures
    Plukked in a ferrë land.

Doun in the Coningere

Bifel that Alys, as on bank she sat
　Hir soster hir besyde, grew wondyr mat,
With naught to doon but twyys piren on
The bok hir soster redde, but peinture non
Ne speche hit nadde, "for what," hir thought, "help is   5
A bok in whiche ne speche ne peinture nis?"

　　Thus then she musëd in hir mynd (to what
Degre she coude, bicause the daye was hat,
And made hir slepi fele, and foltisch eke)
Wher risyng uppe the dayësyes to seke   10
And plukke to make a cheyne that sholdë be
To paye wer worth the werk, when she dyde se
A White Coninge, with ÿes palë red
Sodeynly run, and nigh to hir passëd.

　　This nas nat *over* straunge, nor semëd hit   15
Unnaturel to Alys when the Whit
Coninge she herdë saye, "Alas, alas!

To latë shal I be!" (thogh that hit was
A thyng she oughte have wondred at was clere
When afterward hir thought of hit, but there   20
Hit semëd ben ful naturel) but when
The Coninge *toke an astrolabë* then
Veraili *from his male,* and gan the hour
Espie, and hasten on in sori stour,
Alys lept uppe, for sodeynly in mynd   25
She had that never erst ne myght she fynd
A coninge with a male, or astrolabe
To take from hit, ne herde man therof blabbe,
And brennyng hot with curiositë
Over the feld to folwen hit ran she   30
In godë tyme to seen hit duven doun
A coningere, binethe a heggë broun.

Next minute doun went Alys aftyr hit,
Warloker to have wrought had shown more wit,
For she ne woot ne carëd for hir peine   35
How she of that quarterne sholde com ageyn.
Streight lyk a tonel went the coningere,
Then dipped doun when hit had goon thus fere,
So sodeynly that Alys might not thenche
Betime to stop ere she cam in that trenche,   40
Whiche semëd to hir lyk a ful depe welle,
And hedlinge into hit than Alys felle.
Aither the welle was depe, or doun she went
Ful slowly, for long space had she on bent
To loke about, and wonder what shal nexte   45
Befallen hir. Of that she redde no texte,
For alle was derk binethe wher she sholde come.
Then on the wellës sidës saw she some
Pressës and bokë schelves, and here and ther
Hangyng on peggës mappamoundës wer.   50
Peinturës eke she saw, and from a schelf
Toke as she passed a bottel for hir self
That *Orange Confit* on a label bore,
But found that in hit was, alas, namore.
She nolde hit droppe for fere some wight to quelle   55
That stod binethe, so put hit as she felle
Within a presse she passëd by that tyde.
[A thyng of wight, what ellës may bityde,
As lernëd men, filosophers, do seyn
(Rede Chaucer: *Hous of Famë* maketh pleyn),   60
By kyndëly enclynyng algate shal
His kyndely stedë seken, and doun fall—
But Alys niste the bottel nolde arrive
At botme soner than sholde she on lyve,
And therfor nas nat perilous that tyde.]   65

"Forsooth," quod Alys, "now this falle besyde
To tumblen stayrë doun shal seme no fors,
And alle at home shal thench me strong as hors!
I noldë sey a word though that I flewe
From top of hous!" (Whiche doutëlees was trewe.)   70
    Doun, doun, doun. Sholde hir fallyng never end?
"How manie myl, I wonder, have I wend,"
Quod she aloud, "by now? I moot be nigh
To middel erthës middel, so from high
To depthis have I come. As I me minne,   75
Four thousand myl is this the erthe withinne."
[Had she of Dantë herde, and who was pighte
So depe in erthe, she had ben lesse wel dighte!]
(Manie suche thyngës, understondeth ye,
At schole, as gramer and geometrë,   80
She lernt; though now hir conninge to display
With none to here was not best tyme, assay
She wolde to help remembren hem.) "Wel right
That distantz semeth, but I wonder myght
What Latitude or Almicantëras   85
I have com to?" (What Latitudë was
Or Almicantëras niste Alys nought,
But grand the wordës wer to seyn, hir thought.)
    She sone bigan ageyn. "Perchance I shall,
I wonder wel, right *thurgh* the erthë fall!   90
And com out straungë folk emong, wher men
With heddës up-so-doun methinketh ren
In the Antiphoners." (She somdel glad
At *this* stound was that no one herde: she drad
The word was wrong.) "But nedës most I aske   95
What cuntrë I am in, nor fere the taske.
'Miladi, praye, is this lond Taprobon?
Perchance is hit the lond of Prester John?'"
(To bowen curteislye she triëd as

She spoke—though fallyng thurgh the ayre she was: 100
Thench ye ye coude?) "How ignorant a mayde
If I sholde aske she shal me deme," she sayde.
"Best not to aske. Perchance the name is writ
Upon som bord to saye what lond is hit."
Doun, doun, doun. Alys coude naught ellës do,   105
So sone bigan to talk ageyn. "Also
Shal Dinah muchë missen me to-night,
Methinketh!" (Dinah was the namë right
Of Alys cat.) "I hope for any thyng
Hir platter milk at soper tyme they bryng.   110
Dinah, my dere! I wissh the here with me!
No mise ben in the ayre, I fere, but se,
Perchance thou mayest cacche a rerëmus:
A flindermus, thou canst, is lyk a mus.
But eten cattës bakkës?" Alys here   115
Grew drusi, and, as though she dremyng were,
Went on and on, "Ete cattës bakkës?" or
Sum tymës "Eten bakkës cattës?" for,
Syn nother questioun ne coude she answer,
No fors whiche way she dyde hit round transfer.   120
Softly on slepe she glode, and sone she met
That hand in paw with Dinah walked she yet
And ernestly dyde aske, "Now, Dinah, say
Me sooth, didst ever ete a bakke, or nay?"
When with a sodeyn flap she camë doun   125
Upon an hepe of stikkes and levës broun
And with that flap hir fall was at an end.
     Hooli unhurt she was, and sone gan wend.
In hast she lepëd uppe. Alle overhed
Was derke, but hir bifore a passage led   130
Wher stil in sight the White Coningë ran.
No minute lost awei went Alys than,
As swift as wind, and as hit tornëd past

An herne she herde hit saye in voys agast,
"Hoo, by min erës and the herës by   135
My nosëthirles, how late hit is I spy!"
Though nigh she was, beyond the herne she found
That hit was gone, and she hir self on ground
Within a longe lowe hall, with lampës lit
That hangynge from the rof enlumined hit.   140
    The dorës doun the hall wer lokkëd alle;
She walked along one sydë doun the halle
And uppe that other, tryyng every dore,
Then sadly doun the middel, wondryng sore
How she myght ever comen oute ageyn.   145
    Then sodeynly a table she was fayn
To find, of solide glas, with leggës thre,
And litel gylden kei theron, that she
Hopëd myght ope som dore along the halle.

The lokkës wer to large, or kei to smalle,   150
Alas! hit fitted noon. The nexte tyme round
A lowë cortin not seen ere she found,
Behynde whiche was, som fiftene inches high,
A litel dore: to this she gan draw nigh
And in the lok she set the litel kei   155
Of gold. With joye she found hit fitte, parfey!
    Alys opëd the dore and saw hit led
Into a passage smal as ratouns hed;
She knelëd doun and lokëd hit along
Into a gardyn soote with briddes song   160
And flourës bright and cristal wellës clere
That *locus amoenus* wel might hit appere.
She longëd goon to hit from that derke halle,
But myght not poke hir hed in overalle.
"And even *wolde* hit thurgh the dore," hir thought,   165
"Withoute my schuldren aftyr hit ybrought,
Of litel us that were. In feith I wisshe
That I myght shrink, al wer hit ful foltisshe,
And folden lyk a pedlers empti bagge,
Or silken cloth; per cas I might, I brag,   170
Knewe I but how I myght beginne." Seestow,
So manie straungë thinges had happëd now
That fewe thynges impossíblë semed to hir.
    To wayten by the dore and not to stir
Of no us semed, so to the tablë bak   175
She went, with half a hope hit sholde not lak
Another kei, or bok to reulen how
A wight shal folden lyk a bagge, and now
She found a litel botel on hit (that
"Nas ther bifore, as brook I wel min hat!"   180
Quod Alys). Tyëd to the botels nek
A paper label was, that hir gan chek,
With 𝔇𝔯𝔶𝔫𝔨𝔢 𝔪𝔢 writ in lufly lettrës large.

As knight that noldë juste withoute a targe
In hast nolde wisë litel Alys drink,   185
Though "drynke me" bade hit, for "I sholde forthynk
Hit sorely if I dyde not loke to se
If 'poysoun' on the bottel written be;"
For manie merie talës had she red
Of children brent, by wildë beestës fretëd,   190
Or by other dethës ded, for that
They *nolde* rememberen in no wise what
The simple reulës were hir freendz had taught:

Exempli gratia, the hot end raught
Of eny stikke in fyr pokëd shal bren   195
The sore if over long thou holde hit then,
And if *ful* depe thy finger thou sholde kitte,
Hit bledeth, generally; she nolde forgite
That if from bottel merkëd "poysoun" thow
Muche drinke, hit shal the tenë, late or now.   200
    This bottel *nas* not "poysoun" merkëd, so
Alys durst tast hit. Sone she wantëd mo:
(Freshë flavor hit had of chiries soote,
With blancmange mengëd, appel, spicëd roote,
And rostëd swan and wastel bredes fyne)   205
And schortlye of this liquor made she fyne.

*   *   *   *
*   *   *
*   *   *   *

"How coryouse!" she cryde, for with the drink
She felt hire straungëly begin to shrink,
As foldeth blosme when goth sonne to rest,
Or clothës Abigail wol schutte in chest.   210
Ten inches high she was, and smilëd bright,
Bicause hir thought she was of lencthë right
To intren at the lowë dore and walk
Into the gardyn, grene with lefe and stalk,
And aiwher swete with flourës as whanne Eve   215
Abreyde in Eden, as we boke bileve.
But fyrst she wayted lest she shrynken myght
Som more, and in the end lyk candel lyght
Go oute: somdel aferde she wondred sore
How she sholde felë whanne she was no more.   220
She niste, for never myght she se the leme
When she blew candels oute, how hit sholde seme.

When no more happëd she determinëd
To interen the gardyn withoute dred;
But at the dore, alas! pore Alys found   225
She had the gylden kei foryit that stound,
And at the table myght not recchen hit
By possibilitë, though hit dyde sit
In pleyn sighte thurgh the glas, ne myght she clim
The tablë for to sliper was ech lim;   230
And when she weri was with tryyng, pore
Alys sat sadly wepyng by the dore.
  "To wepen thus accomplisseth right naught!"
She somdel scharpely toold hirself, "the aught,
By min avis, this minute stop!" Oft gave   235
She gode avis (but seldë wolde hit have),
Sum tymës scoldëd hir so fersly that
Into hir yës cam the terës hat,
And onys tried hir owën eres to box
Bicause she had deceyuëd hir, as fox   240
Doth cok that crowë shal with yës schutte,
When hir ageynst she pleyëd at the putte:
Hit lyked this straungë child pretenden two
She were. "That serveth naught pretenden so,"
Pore Alys thought, "for scarcely is enow   245
One hendë wight to maken of me now."
  Binethe the tablë sone she saw of glas
A litel box which when hit opëd was
A smalë cake she found therin, **Ete me**
In reisins fynly writ on hit. Quod she,   250
"This wol I ete, and if I bigger grow
I cheven can the kei, if smal enow
I can crepe under dore; ech wey I shall
The gardyn gayn: I care not what befall!"

A litel pece she ete, and warily   255
"Which wey? Which wey?" she seyde, as carfully
Hir hand on hed she held to fele which way
She grew. Straunge semëd hit that she gan stay
The samë highte; as generally shal hap
When eteth man a cake, but at a clap   260
So manie straungë thynges had Alys seen
That dul hit semëd if hir lyf sholde been
As comunly hit was, so she bigoon
To werke, and sone the cake enter was goon.

      *   *   *   *
         *   *   *
    *   *   *   *

Chapitre II

The Pol of Teres

edeth anon how Alys and a mus   265
    That fyrst hir thought was an ypotamus
With sundri briddes and straunge beestes swam
That with hem in a pol of teres cam,
For whan in Wondyr Lond she ete the cake
She grew so large she wepte a large lake.   270
    "Coryouser curiuser!" Alys cryde,
Astonied so she lat gode Englyssch slyde,
"Now lyk a *trébuchet*, that whirleth high
A stone, I fele me reche the welkne nigh!
Farewel my feet!" So far of dyde they seme   275
She had smal sight of hem hir ye to queme.
"Some other wight, my deres, most tye on
For you your hoses, and do on your shoon!
I may not bowe so fer my feet to reche
To doon hem wonted servys, nay, so thee'ch!   280
Bihoveth me be kind, or they wol walk
In opposition to the waye I talk!
Ech yer at Youle, bi cause I may not bend,

Newe shoos by messager shal I moot send,
As yiftes, under sele of lettres lele   285
With superscripture writ to tos and hele:

> *'My lord right fot,*
> *upon the reedi flore,*
> *Besyde the fyr,*
> *(with Alys love grete store).'*

This tale," quod she, "is of waltrot!"
    and tyte
She felt hir hed agayns the roof-
    bemes smyte.   290
Nine fot and more in highte she was,
    pardee,
The litel table lower than hir knee.
    Swiftly the gylden key from of the
    glas
She toke, and strad to wher the
    gardyn was.
Pore Alys scarcely when on syde she
    laye   295
With an ye piren myght wher she
    wolde playe.
No hope of interyng she nadde, and
    on
The flore she sat and wepte agayn ful
    won.
    Than contritely she sayde, "Thee
    hoveth schame
So large as thou"—she wel deserved
    that name—   300
"So strangly wepen! I sey stop right
    now!"

Hir teres natheles continued flow
As from a spigot in a tun had swepte
A depe flod round hir, for galouns she wepte.
Four inches depe, half doun the halle hit ran.   305
To drye hir yes she in hast began:
A tapping that she herde of feet foretoold
The comyng of the White Coninge boold.
Huf! A galonte! Proudly dressed was he,
Alys disesperat for help was she.   310

Gloves of kidz wulle and a large fan
He bore, "The Duchesse!" moteryng as he ran:
"Wood wrath the Duchesse for defaute of me
Shal chide, I drede, for loth to wayte is she."
Than timorously Alys spak, "Sir, help!"   315
The Coninge sprang, and as she were a whelp
Cast fanne and gloves doun and fled as tyte
Into the derke as man had lost his wit.
    She toke the fanne to cool hir chekes hot,
And as she talked used hit: "I not,"   320
Quod she, "so coryouse as thinges bene
To-day, so unlyc yisterday, I wene,
If sodeynly I chaunged in the night?
Was I the same when I by morwenyng light
Abreyde? Methinketh I remember can   325
I somdel different felte. Who am I than?"
She cast in mynd the children that she knewe
Of hir yonge age, if she was torned trewe
To one of hem. "I nam not Ada, no,
Whose haire is long and crulle, but min not so;   330
Nor myght I silly Mabel be, the fol:
She knoweth lite, but I can al I wol.
But *she* is she, and *I* am I—parfey,
How hit beguileth me! I shal assay
What I coude formerly of arsmetrike,   335
Orbis terrarum, or of rhethorique.
IV timës V is XII, that is no nay,
IV timës VI XIII, the sooth to say,
IV timës VII—what is that the som?
Alas, to XX shal I never com!   340
I do no fors of multiplicatioun!
Than lat me speke of cuntre, stowe and toun.
Roma capud—of Paris pope is king
And London is the newe Babelynge.

Alas, I moot be Mabel, ye, certayn! 345
But clom! Lat heere the cukkow song agayn."
  With handes in hir lap she made a croys
But sayde wrong wordes in a straunge hors voys:

> Winter is ycumen in 348a
> Softe sing cukkow
> Fadeth sede and drinketh mede
> The joly craftmon now
>   Sing thou cukkow!

> Loweth after bule the cow 348f
> Myrie singeth owl now
> Ewe bleteth swine freteth
> Everichoon sing cukkow now
>   I and thou, I and thou,
>   I and thou cukkow! 348k

"Thise woordes ben not right," she sayde and wepte.
"Mabel forsooth I am, and shal be kepte 350
In narwe cotage, with a hen or two,
And swich a hepe of werk al daye to do!
If I be she, I set me to remayn
In coni clapper, and not com up agayn.
My folk may put hir heddes doun and say 355
'Alys com up!' for naught, for I shal stay,
And oonly aske, 'Who am I then? For til
Ye telle me, and me liketh that wight gentil,
I com not up til som wight els I be!'
But oute, alas, I wisshe that I myght se 360
Hir heddes, here aloon is drery fare."
  Thus wepyng Alys sayde. She wurth aware
The Coninges white litel glove she wore
"An impossīblë, but to fit the dore

I growë lesse," quod she, and went to mete   365
Hir by the table, wher in highte two feet
She demed she was, and swiftly yet forschrank.
Had she not dropt the fanne, upon that plank
She had ben gone, as morning mist at none.
  Escaped hardly thus, and not to sone,   370
But wel apayd that yet on lyf she was,
She soght the gardyn dore, the floures and gras,
But hit was schutte, and hie on table lay
Agayn the key. "Alas and weilaway!
Unhap is al," she sayde, "quaad last I bere   375
For never syn my birthe so smal I nere!"

  Sodeynly slypte hir fot, and with a plasche
Chin-depe in salten water dyde she dasche.
"Be this the se," hir thought, "on shipbord may
I home retorn, for wel I woot a kei   380
Wher marchaunts wont descenden in ech port
Of Engelond stont." (Onys for hir disport

Had Alys sene the se, and shippes thought
Continuely riche chaffare hamward brought,
Or soudeurs sent to maken war in Fraunce,   385
Or folk on pilgrimage, to lerne the daunce
To se Seint Jame, or Rome, or cloistre hem
With monkes livynge in Ierusalem.)
Nathles, she sone persawe in pol she swam
Of teres she had wepte with litel scham   390
When nine fot high. "I wisshe," quod she, "I nadde
So plentevously wepte," and wondred sadde
How she might win to schore. "How straunge to be
Punisched by my superfluitee
To drown in teres!" Alys sayde, "but alle   395
Semeth but straunge today that me befalle."
    A plaschinge in the pol she herde, and ner
Hit swam to se what slypped had in ther:
Hir thought the noys bitokened, per cas,
Ypotamus or whal! but saw hit was   400
Naught but a mus, rememberyng how smal
She was bicom. What boot if she sholde cal
To hit and sholde assaye if hit coude speke?
"Can ye, O Mus," she asked lowe and meke
For in hir brothers donat stod hit thus   405
"Mus, muses, to a mus, a mus, O mus,"
Al wer not maydens Latyn wont to lere,
"Can ye, O Mus, the passage oute from here?
Taedium vitae—no, *natandi*, me
Sore greveth!" Never ere with mise spak she,   410
But *casus vocativus* hir thought right,
As sayde the bok wherof she had had sight.
Inquisitif hit loked, but no word sayde
But semed as hit winked on the mayde.
    "Englysch to hit sans doute is ful unknowe,   415
Hit speketh Frensche of Stratford-atte-Bowe!

From Normandie hit cam with Guillaume King
And Conquerour"—of tyme she knewe no thyng—
"Où est ma chatte?" So had she lered say
In Babees bok. The Mus in grete affray   420
Out of the water sprang and tremblyng stode.
"*Mea culpa!*" Alys cryde, who understode
She had distourbed sore the beest that joye
None had of cattes, but ful muche anoye.
"An ye wer me," the Mus cryde loude and shrille,   425
"Sholde *ye* lyke cattes, with hir yvel wille?"
"Nay, I foryeve yow youre ire, and yet
Dinah my cat I trow, an ye hir met,
Wol plese yow, so dere and stil she is,"
Quod Alys gentilly, "tak kepe of this,"   430
As idly in the pol about she swam,
"So fond of Dinah ye may gess I am,
That sitteth by the fyr, and licketh wrists
To wasshe hir face betwix hir deyntee fists,
So softe to norisse in min armes she is   435
And swift to clawen and to cacchen mys—"
For fere and ire the Muses haire upbrayd,
"A, *mea culpa!*" Alys sorhful sayd,
"We wole not speke of Dinah an ye nole."
"We?" cryde the Mus, from hed to footes sole   440
And end of tail tremblyng, "Nay, of that
I nolde never speke! I *hate* a cat!
Stinkynge and vile they ben, as is a tord!
So thenke my family eke: we hate the word!"

  "No moore of that," sayd Alys hastyflye,   445
"But whelpes ye may luven naturally."
She went on, for non answere made the Mus,
"A joly whelp that dwelleth nigh oure hus
I wolde yow show, with eyen bryght and haire
Crulle brune, that wol fecchen stykkes faire,   450

And sit and beg whan hit wol dine, or seche
For other thing of which me fayleth speche.
A yeman oweth hit: for hundred pound,
His maister seith, nil he at ony stound
This worthy whelp to whomsoever selle   455
So radly hit in berne can rattes quelle."

    With that the Mus as hard as hit myght go
Swam of, and lat the pol plasche to and fro.
"Marie!" quod Alys in a sorhful voys,
"I have afered hit agayn, by choys.   460
Dere Mus, com bak, and noght of cat ne whelp
An ye lyk not we speke so ye me help!"
    With pale face the Mus swam slowly bak.
"Lat swim us to the schore of this wet lak,"
Hit al a-trembel sayd, "and why so loth   465
I ben of dogges and of cattes both
I shal yow wisse." Hie tyme it was to go
So grete a croud of beests and briddes tho
Wer in the pol yfalle. A Dok, a gaye
Phoenix, a Tercel and a Papengaye   470
And more of straunge ther wer. Alys hem led,
And broght hem al to schore, withouten dred.

CHAPITRE III

A Concilie-Rese and a Longe Tale

In feith a straunge companye hit was
    That gadred on the bank in woful cas,
The briddes fethers dagged wer and wet,   475
The beestes furre clong clos in wicke jet.
Alle wete, in wrecchedom, ire and discomfort,
They held a parlement, whos chef import
Was how they myght hem drye. In schorte space
Alys was of hir felawschipe, by grace   480
Of nature, as if fostred al hir lyf
Togider. She was argumentatyf
And nolde agreen with the Papengaye
That colrik atte laste wold namoore saye
But "Elder I am thanne thou, and therfore,   485
As night doth folwe daye, of connyng more."
This Alys nolde admitin til she wiste
The Papengayes age, but hit ne liste
Hir wissen, so they helde no forther speche.

At last the Mus, who semed apt to teche,   490
As clerk or maister who hath governaunce,
"Sitteth adoun, and lat me now avaunce,"
Hit cryde, "and herkneth, I shal maken yow,
Certayn, in schorte space drye ynow!"
Without delay they sat doun in a ring,   495
The Mus in midst. Alys for ony thyng
Nolde look awei, for fere that in hir nose
But she grew swiftly drye sholde be the pose.
    "Hem!" sayde the Mus in maner real, "be
Ye redi? Pes, and herkneth unto me.   500
Silence I pray, and ye shal here a thing,
The driest that I knowe I shal yow bring.

> 'Guillaume of Normandie to Englond cam   502a
> As Conquerour, with favour of the Pope,
> To teme the Englyssch, who sahtled al sam
> For want of duces. Monie nobles shope
> To conquer and usurp as they had hope
> To win, til Edwin erle of Mercia
> And mihti Morcar of Northumbria—'"   502g

    "A!" quod the Papengaye and chivered
As though to beg to ben delivered.
    "I praye thee of grace," cortayslye sayde   505
The Mus, though hit a frouning frount displayde,
"But dydst thou speke?" The Papengaye in haste
Nikked him nay. "Methought thou dydst. Hold faste!

> 'Edwin and Morcar, to continue on,   508a
> The erles, as I sayde, of Mercia
> And eke ye wiste, be not youre wittes gone
> A blakeberied, Northumbria,
> Bicom his men from here to Asia,

So likewise Stigand, archebischop nice
Of Caunterbury, found hit gode avys—'"   508g

"Found *what?*" enquered the Doke. "Found *hit*,"
Answerde the Mus in som anoy, "Ye wit   510
Forsooth what meneth 'hit,' I trowe!" "Yis,"
Answerde the Doke, "I knowe what meneth this
Whanne *I* fynde ought, a froske I have in mynd,
Or els a wyrm—what dyde the bischop fynde?"
This question the Mus was loth to here   515
And onward dyde his drery spekyng stere.

"'The archebischop found hit gode avys   516a
That he sholde goon with Edgar Atheling
And offer Guillaume Conquerour, iwis,
The croune. Help was there noon but make him King.
His rule at fyrst was not a hevie thyng
But sone the pryde and bobbaunce of his men—'"   516f

The Mus askt Alys if by proces then   516g
She feled drye at last. "No whit," sayde she
In sorhful voys, "ne dryeth hit not me."
     "Syn that is so," the Phoenix sayde, and ros
Solempnely and stode upon his tos,   520
"I juge this parlement ajourne at ones,
And remedies effectyf for the nones
Undertake—" "Englyssch speke!" the Tercel cryde,
I noot what meneth half thise termes wyde
And over more ne leeve I that ye can   525
Hem also." Thanne the Tercel bent his pan
To hide a smile; som other briddes lough.
The Phoenix thus offended made hit tough,
And sayde, "I wolde have bidden that we renne
A concilie-rese, we shal drye soner thenne."   530

"What *is*," quod Alys, "a concilie-rese?"
She dyde no cure to knowe, but for to plese
The Phoenix spake, for hit had semed to pause
To answere ony question in a clause,
That *som* wight, hit had thought, moot aske, parfey, 535
But oonly Alys willing was to say.

    "Of that," the Phoenix sayde, "best is to doon."
(Now herkneth, al and som, for ye may goon
About to doon hit on a wintrys daye
I shal expoun the Phoenix' maner playe.) 540

     To merke the cours a cercle rough hit drewe
("No nede ther is," hit seyde, "to merk more trewe,")
Then put the parti here and there along
The cours. No word awayted, on they throng
As liked hem, and stopped rennyng whan 545
Hit semed gode and thus hir rese they ran.
Whan hit sholde end not esi was to spye,
But after half an hour whan alle were drye
In sodeyn wise the Phoenix bade hem "Hold!
The rese is doon!" They crouded round hit, bold 550
And panting. "Who hath won?" Hit thoughte long
And made a poynting with his finger strong
[The Phoenix had a finger: see the hand
Binethe his wing depicted on the wand]
(Ye knowe how maister Chaucer is depeynt 555
By Hawes, poynting as he were a seynt.)
Alle wayted wordles, til the Phoenix wise
Sayde "*Alle* have won, and *alle* most win a prise!"
A quere of voyces tho gan crye, "Who shal
Give oute the prises?" "She, biside this wal," 560
The Phoenix sayde, with poynt indicatyf
Of Alys, who knewe not, upon hir lyf,
What was at do, as al that motlee crewe
Descending round hir "Prises" cryde anewe.

Alys at dulcarnon and in despeire 565
Found in hir male a box of confyts feire,
Not wete, as Fortune wolde, in nomber just,
The which she handed round to eches lust.
"But she hirself moot have a pris," the Mus
Declared. "Ye, forsooth," the Phoenix thus 570
Ful sobrely agreed, and asked Alys
"What other thyng withinne thy male here is?"
"Noght but a thimbel," Alys sadly siyed.
"Gif me hit here," the Phoenix stern replied.

They crouded round agayn. Solempnely 575
The Phoenix with thise others faste by
Profred the thimbel thus: "We praye yow,

Accepteth," quod the Phoenix, "this gifte now
And take hit for a jewel." To conclude
His schorte speche the meynie shouted loude.   580
    Alys for folie took the dede, but they
With sobre chere; she durst not lough or playe,
And liste not speke, but humbly bowed lowe
And toke the thimbel with solempne showe.

    Thanne was hit tyme the confyts soote to ete   585
Which caused tene: the large briddes plete
They coude not tasten hires, and to choke
The smale ones gan, and blowes toke,
To help hem, on the bak, til atte last
Al they wer wel and sat hem doun in hast   590
In fourme of cercle that the Mus myght telle
A thyng or two they list to heren welle.

    "Mus, thou bihotest me thin historie
To telle, why thou hatest—C and D,"
Whispered Alys, lest she might ageyn   595
Offenden hit. The Mus with mighte and mein
Siyed and sadly torned him to Alys.
    "A long and ful sadde tale," quod hit, "min is."
    "A longe tail hit *is* certaynly that,"
Sayde Alys, lokyng doun in wunder at   600
The Muses tail, "but wherfore saystow sadde?"
"No resoun is," hir thoughte, "but if thou madde."
Thurghoute the Muses speche she wondred more
Of this and herde of hit but litel store.
His trewe wordes dyde she algate mis,   605
The soun she herde was somwhat lyk to this:—

"Furre sayde
  to a mus,   606a
    That he met
      in the hus,   606b
        'Lat us both
          go to lawe: *I*
            shal appel-
              en *yow*.—   606c
            Come, ye
            shal not
              denyë,   606d
            The case we
          moot tryë,   606e
        sooth is it so
      this mor-
      wen noght
      have I
      at do.'   606f
        Sayde the
          mus to
            the hound,   606g
              'Such a
                case sholde
                  be found,   606h
                    With no
                    jurre or
                    juge a
                  wast of
                    oure breth.   606i
                  'I shal
                  be Juge
                I shal
              be Jurre,'   606j
              sayde
              cun-
                ning
                  old
                    Furre: 606k
                      'I
                      shal
                        trye
                        al
                      the
                    cas,
                  and
                deme
                yow
              to
            deth.'   606l

"Thou merkst me not!" the Mus gan sternely saye
To Alys. "Wher wente thi wittes oute to playe?"
  "A, *mea culpa*," humbly answered she,
"Biside the fifte bend methought ye be."   610

"Nay, that then*k not*" the irous Mus upbreyde.

"A knotte!" cryde Alys, swift with help purveyde,
"Wher is hit? Lat me help untye hit sone!"

"Nay verily, that shal I nawhit done,"
In answere quod the Mus and strad awei.   615
"Such daffy speche scorneth me, I saye!"

    Pore Alys gan to plete hit wolde remayne
"Ye take so swift offense now agayn!"
The Mus naught sayde but "Grr!" "Plese yow com bak
And let us of your storie fin not lak,"   620
Cryde Alys after hit. The othres alle
"Yis, Mus, plese do!" togidres gan to calle.
Dispitously the Mus but schoke his hed,
And gan to walken faster fro that sted.

    "Alas that hit nolde stay," the Papengaye   625
Siked, whan hit was oute of sight awaye.

An olde Crabbe whan she sawe hir tyme
Unto hir doghter sayde, with chere grim,
"My dere, lerne fro this to wrathe *thee* never!"
"I wolde to holde thi tonge thou hadde lever,   630
Moder," the yonge Crabbe fersly cryde
That frouned a litel bi hir modres syde,
"I nam no nonne to bide alwey in cloistre,
And take hit al in patience lyk an oistre!"

   "I wissche," quod Alys, heere hir myght who leste,   635
"Dinah wer here: hit sone sholde *she* areste!"

   "And who is Dinah," quod the Papengaye,
"If I so bold a question aske maye?"

   Egrely Alys answered tho, for she
Of talk about hir cat was alwey free: 640
"Dinah is oure cat, and sovereign
To cacchen mys, and dooth hir besy peine
To renne after briddes. *Bendicite!*
A brid she wolde frete as sone as se!"

   Wonder distourbled wer they by this speche   645
And monie briddes comsed, on and eche,
To hasten foorth. An olde janglyng Pye
Wrapped hir shulder wel and carfullye:
For "Par ma fey!" she sayde, "now taketh note!
I moot go ham, the night wol noye my throte!"   650
A throstil tremblyng cryde, "My children dere
Ye sholde long ere this to bed repere!"
For sundri resouns gan they alle departe
And lafte Alys aloon upon hir parte.

   "I wisshe I nadde of Dinah mencioun made!"   655
Quod she, and looked sorweful and sadde,
"Hit semeth no wight lyketh hire doun here,
Though aller beste cat thou art, my dere,
I noot if I shal ever se thee more!"

Tho gan pore Alys wepe, and wepte ful sore,   660
Aloon and mat. But sone a litel rerde
A tapping as of feet agayn she herde
And looked egrely in hope the Mus
To end his storie was retorned thus.

The Coninge Sendeth
in a Litel Bille

Alys agayn the White Coninge saw,   665
  Trotting bak slow, and serching with his paw
For somthyng loste, and moteringe "The Duchesse!
A, the Duchesse!" in wo and hevinesse,
"My dere paws, mine heires and my furre,
Bihefded at commaunde of hir past cure   670
Mine hap shal be, as certayn as fyrettes
Been fyrettes: no more of me thou gettes!
Wher dropt I hem, I wonder?" At a gesse
Alys divined of his grete distresse
That hit had lost the gloves and the fan,   675
And kindely as resoun was bigan
To serche for hem, but nowher myght hem se,
For aftyr in the tery pol swam she
Had come a chaunge, hit semed, over alle.
Vanesched was al outrely the halle   680
With glasi table and the litel dore:

No sight of hem remayned ony more.
    Ful sone the Coninge Alys serchyng found,
"What *dostow* Marianne upon this ground?"
In angri voys hit cryde, "renne ham at ones   685
And fecche me fan and gloves for the nones!"
Alys was so afered that she ran
The waye hit with his finger showen gan,
And wayted not his errour to expoun.
    "He thenketh me his houskepare, boun   690
To serve him," Alys sayde, hwiles that
She ran, "ful wel astonied, my hat
To borwe, shal he felen whan he fynt
I nam not she! But now, bifore I stynt,
Myght I hem fynde, his gloves and his fan   695
I shal bitake to him." With that she gan
Bihoold a tidy litel hus. The dore
Upon a plate of bras the name bore
𝔴. 𝒞𝑜𝓃𝒾𝓃𝑔𝑒. Ne knokked she but went
In up the stayre in hast lest she be sent   700
Awei bifore she myght the gloves get
If she the trewe Marianne met.
    "Hit semeth straunge to been a messagere
Servyng a coninge in a coningere,"
Quod Alys. "Nexte shal Dinah as may be   705
'Go bet, and doon this erande!' saye to me!"
And thought in fantasie how hit myght hap:
"'Milady Alys, com as tyte and wrap
Thi mantel on, for tyme hit is to ride!'
'A moment, norice, first I moot abyde   710
Biside this mushole lest the mus com oute,
Til Dinah shal retorne!' But yet I doute
Mi folk nolde kepen Dinah if she leste
To send us alle on erandes at hir heste!"

Bi this within a tidi chambre she   715
Was come, and bi the window saw with gle
A table that as she had hoped bore
A fan and, such as curteoures wore,
White gloves smale, peires two or thre:
An paire gloves and the fan toke she.   720
As she aboute to leeve the chambre was
She saw a botel by the lokunge bras.
No legend bade 𝖣𝗋𝗒𝗇𝗄𝖾 𝗆𝖾, but nathelesse
She toke the stoppel out, and drank. "I gesse,"
Quod she, "som chaunge coryouse shal fal,   725
As whan I ete, or drynke a cordial.
Lat se this botel if hit doth me grow:
Ful loth I am to been so litel now."
        In sooth hit dyde, and soner than hir thought,
She had not drunk the half before hit brought   730
Hir hed agaynst the roof, and she most bend,
Or breke hir nek. She lat the botel wend,
"Of that ynow, I hope I grow no more,"
Quod she, "algate I may not passe the dore—
In feith, I wissche I nadde drunk so muche!"   735
        To late, alas! hit was to wisschen suche
A thyng as that she ought have drunken lesse.
Swiftly she grew and grew, in soothfastnesse,
Til on the flore perforce she moste knele
But in a minute while bothe hed and hele   740
Flatlinge adoun she layde upon the flore;
Hir elbowe pressed was agaynst the dore,
Hir oother arm she crulled round hir hed,
But stil she grew, as if of geaunts bred.
Hir fot she threste up chimnee sauf from harm,   745
And at the wyndow out she putte hir arm.
"This al and som, I can no more, hap what
May hap," quod she, "I se no end of that."

Bon chance! The magik naturel that in
The botel hoved now had recched fin: 750
She grew not larger, but ful confortlesse
Hir prisoun was, and eke she myght not gesse
If she sholde oute ageyn. A, if Alys
Ful wo and wrecched was no wonder is.

"At ham," hir thought, "I lyved faire and welle,   755
Not up and doun as bucket in a welle,
And toold, 'Do this!' by mys and coninges.
Al most I wissche I nadde nat gone, I ges,
Doun in the coningere, and yet this lyf
Parfay is coryouse! I wonder yf   760
A ferly me bifell, of fayerye
Ywrought, that I was wont to deme folye
But in a romaunce here I am! Of me
Bihoveth hit a bok be writ, pardee,
Which when grown up I shal myself endite   765
In vers for choys, in vers I wol hit write
For drasty prose I give not a russhe;
My makyng shal 'The Aunters of—' but hushe!

I am wel grown," she sayde in wrecchednesse,
"Here nis no roume to grow, I can confesse!   770
But if I may not grow I may not elde
And never for an olde vekke be helde—
That doth me gladden—a, but then, alas,
Alweis to lerne: in that is no solas!"
    Then answer made she to hirself, "O fol,   775
In this place is scars roume to put thi pol
And none for ony bok on which to lere!"
    So to and fro she spake and thanne gan here
A voys binethe the window. Hir debat
She stopped, and gan herken what was that.   780
    "Marianne, Marianne!" the voys sayde, "fecche me
My gloves cof, as tyte, in blink of ee!"
Feet tapped on the stayre, and Alys knewe
The Coninge wolde hir seke. Aferde anewe
She trembled til the hool hous schoke, iwis,   785
Foryetyng she a thousand tyme by this
Was larger than the Coninge, and of hit
No resoun was for fere. Hit cam as tyte
And made assaye to intren at the dore,
But therat Alys elbowe pressed sore: 790
Into the chambre myght hit nowise come.
Then Alys herde hit saye, "This al and some,
"I shal thenne at the window climben in!"
    "Ye, haselwode! Thou shalt not herein win,"
Thought Alys, wayting til hir thought she herde   795
That clos binethe the window hit had ferde;
She spredde hir hand oute sodeynly, and made
A snacche in ayre. She no thyng gode ne badde
Ne caught, but herde a scriche and fall: ther came
The soun of brekyng glas, as from a frame   800
Wher cucumers wer grown: the Coninge fat
Peraventure had fallen into that.

Nexte cam an angri voys, the Coninges:
"Wher artow, Andrew, losel? What thynges
Dostow?" Alys then herde a newe nois,   805
From country fer bi north, a straunge voys:
"Diggand for appels, sir, and werkand here!"
    "*Digging* for appels?" angrily came answere,
"Com hither, helpe me from this sory pas!"
(Ther cam a soun of moore brekyng glas.)   810

"Now telle me, Andrew, what in window is?"
"Datheit wha kens, an arum, sir, iwis!"
"A gos thou art! No arm can be so large!
Hit filleth al the window lyk a targe!"
    "Ay, sa it dois, sir, but it is an arum!"   815
"What that hit be, hit doth no gode but harm!
Go bet, and lok thou take hit wel awei!"
    To this no answer Alys herde him saye,
But whispres now and then, as, "Na, I lyk
It nat, nicht guid but drublie, ded or quyk!"   820
"Do as I telle thee, craven couard hine!"
    She spradde hir hand agayn to snacche or rine,
Two litel scriches this tyme folwed and
The soun of brekyng glas binethe hir hand.
"How manie cucumers in frames there   825
Most be," thought Alys, "in this coningere!
What nexte, I wonder? Wolde they assaye
To pulle me thurgh the window? *I* nolde staie
Here longer, and I wisshe *they hadde* the might!"
    She wayted til she herde a rombling slight   830
Of litel cart-wheels, and confusioun
Of voyses as at Babel was the soun.
"A nother laddre? Nay, I brought but an!"
"Bille hath that oother." "Fecche hit, Bille, man!"
"Put hem at the corner." "First shaltow tye   835
The twayn togidre that they recchen hie."
"Shal that do wel?" "Ye, hit is lang ynow:
No fors if lakketh hit a fot, I trow!"
"Holde, Bille, this rope!" "Mighte the rof bere wight?"
"Be war that lose slat that fallen myght!"   840
"Hit cometh doun! Ho, hideth heddes!" (Crasshe!)
"Who dyde that?" "Bille!" "Which of you shal dassche
Doun in the chimney?" "Thou?" "Not me!" "Bille tho!"
"Com Bille, the maister seith that thou most go!"

Whan Alys herde pore Bille gat al the werke 845
And moot com doun the chimney streit and derke,
"Neveradel," she sayde, "I envie Bille!
This fireherth narwe is, but kicke I wille."

She drewe hir fot fer doun the
chimney than,
And wayted til a litel schraping
gan 850
To scrattin in the place above.
"Lat se,
If this is Bille, what animal hit
be,"
She sayde, and kicked sharpe.
"Ther goeth Bille!"
A quer of voyces cryde loude and
schrille.
"Hoo! Cacche him, thou that
stondest bi the hegge," 855
She herde the Coninge bid, "his
lyf n'abregge,
But hold his hed up." "Give him
wine, for joye!"
"Nay, choke him not!" "He hath
ynogh!" "My boye,
What hap befell thee saye in
woordes fewest
How from the chimney in the
ayre thou flewest." 860
A litel feble squekyng voys at
last,
"Billes," thought Alys, sayde, "I
noot what cast
Me forth—no more, I thank
yow—I am welle,

But to confus the halvendel to telle.
Methought a dint of thonder dyde me dinge   865
And up I went lyk stones from a slinge!"
　　"In feith thou dydst," they cryde, "as thou wolde roun
With man in mone bifore thou camest doun!"
　　The Coninge sayde, "The hous we moste bren!"
"If that ye do," cryde Alys loude then,   870
"I shal set Dinah on to chasen yow!"
　　At onys al wer stil. "I wonder now,"
Quod Alys, "what they *shal* do nexte? If wit
They had, they wolde uplift the rof as tyt."
Sone Alys herde hem move about agayn,   875
And herde the Coninge say, "This gardin wain
Is ful ynogh, now let begin the play!"
　　"What can be in the wain to make a fray?"
She wundred til smal stones ratled hoot
Upon the window and hir face smoot.   880
"This shal I stop," she sayde, and loude cryde,
"Assaye to shote agayn and bak and syde
Shal Dinah smiten yow!" At onys al
Was stil. No stones hitte agaynst the wal.
　　But sone Alys in wonderment persawe   885
The smale stones bi som magyk lawe
Tornyng to litel cakes on the flore.
"No roum," quod she, "have I to growen more"—
The connyng thought she caught had from this thyng
Som chaunge of mesure etyng hem sholde bring—   890
"So if I eten one, I moot growe lesse!"
　　She swalwed fast, and for hir hardinesse
Gan shrynken til she coude renne doun the stayre
And founde withuten wayting in the ayre
A croude of litel animals and briddes   895
The litel Lesarde Bille hem amiddes.

Two swynes from the sounder held hit up
And gaf hit drink from bottel withoute cup.
To chasen hire at sighte they al bigan
But swiftly to a wode she saufly ran.   900
    Ther as she walked up and doun, hir thoughte
That first hire propre lencth atteyne she oughte
And nexte into the gardyn paradise
Arryve: no bettre plan she myght devyse,
But how she sholde purvei she coude not see.   905

And on a sodeyn, hie biside a tree
A whelp she herde berke above hir hed.
His throte was lyk the fournys of a led
So big hit was, and yet his ye was mild.
Hit straughte his paw to pleyen with the child.   910
"Pore litel thyng!" she sayde in gentil wise
And tryed to whistlen to hit in hire gyse
For much afered she was that hit sholde ete
A litel thyng lyk hire, hit was so grete.

Par aventure she toke a stikke, and threst   915
Hit ner the whelp which lept up so adrest
Hie of the ground, and berkinge with delite
Ran at the stikke as hit the stikke wolde bite.
Alys behind a thistel sprang for fere
Of trampeling, and whan she dyde appere   920
At other syde, hals over heles hit
Tombeled in hast to reche the stikke, sore fit
For Alys! as with cart hors she dyde playe.
In juparde lest his feet hire sholde slaye
She ran aboute the thistel, whil the whelp   925
Ran to and fro; hit neded litel help
To berke and chase the stikke, til atte last
Hit sat with hanging tung and ye half fast.

Than Alys saw hir tyme and ran awei
Til she was mat and brethles, sooth to saye,   930
And dim and fere of whelpes berke herde soun.
"So dere a whelp, hit semeth me resoun,"
Quod she, and lened on a dayesye
To resten hire and cool intentyflye
Hir chekes with a leef for fanne, "to teche   935
Hit wrenches, might I my trewe mesure reche."
But how? "Alas, I hadde nigh foryet
I moot grow up ageyn. How may I get
To right? Suppos I ete or drink som thyng,

But what?" The questioun fayled answering,   940
For though she loked al aboute, no floure
Or leef of gras semed gode for to devoure.
    A grete musseroun of equal highte
To hires nigh hir grew of which the sighte
Binethe and al aboute whan she had take   945
To loke on top she thought she nolde forsake.
Upon the cop right of hire tos she stood
And pired over at the egge abrood.
Ther sat a greet blew catirpel aloon
With armes folden and a longe spoon   950
On which hit suked in his mouth, but nought
Hit noted elles, what per cas hit thought.

CHAPITRE V

Avys from a Catirpel

No word the Catirpel and Alys spak,
But ech at th'other loked long tyme bak
Bifore the Catirpel in sobre wise   955
As hit the juge wer of a greet empryse
Toke from his mouth deliberedly the spoon
That joyned to a pyp thurgh which ther goon
A fire and smoke that blubred in a cup
Alembike that hit semed on to sup—   960
Thus thise filosophres in croslets al
Make gold, and brewe hit for a cordial—
And sluggardly hit sayde, "Who art *thow*?"
    Abasshed bi this shorte speche and slow
Wherby hit dyde not seme to Alys that   965
The Catirpel wolde muche with hir debat,
She scheily answered, "Sir, I niste now,
As at this tyme; in feith, I make a vow,
I can wel who I *was* when I abreyde
This morwenyng, but chaunge," she sadly sayde,   970
"Syn then, I suffred oft, and chaunge ageyn,

Til I what mayde I am to doute am fayn."
  "What menestow by that?" the Catirpel
Demanded sternly. "Say, arecche wel
Thiself!" "*Myself*," quod she, "arecchen may   975
I not, Sir, for, of mercie I yow pray,
I understonden not how hit may be,
But fere I nam myself, as ye may se."

"I se not that," the Catirpel answerde.

"I can not make hit pleyner than ye herde," 980
Quod Alys humbly, "ful confus I saye
Hit is, so many mesures in one daye
To been!" "Hit is not," sayde the Catirpel.

"Perchaunce as yet ye knowe hit not so wel,"
Quod she. "Considereth, when ye chaunge at last, 985
And in a hous of silk most binde yow fast—
Ye shal, for suche is catirpeles lawe
Maugre your pyp and chekes, as we cnawe—
And after that bicom a boterflie,
That ye shal also fele hit strangely." 990

"Nawhit," answerde the Catirpel. "Then ye,"
Quod Alys, "may not fele as I, for *me*
I can wel hit sholde fele straunge!" "For *yow*!"
Hit sayde in scorn, "who artow, I wolde know?"

Thus hadde they bigon hir speche whan 995
They met, as though around a ring they ran.
Such schorte speches sayde hit bi his craft,
A litel ire was in hir herte ylaft.
She stode up streit and sternely sayde, "Ye sholde,
As thynketh me that hit wer bettre tolde, 1000
Disclose, and lat me witen certaynly,
Who *ye* be, first." The Catirpel sayde, "Why?"

This question beguiled hir also,
No gode resoun coude she fynden tho,
And syn so *ful* unfrendli semed his mood 1005
She torned hir awei: hit coude no good.

"Com bak!" the Catirpel calde after hir.
"Of grete import I attle thyng to stir!"
Hir thought this gode, and torned faire and wel.
"Ne wrathe thee not," quod hit, the Catirpel. 1010
"Is that word alle?" she answerde angrily,
But quencht hir ire for hit nas worth a fly.

"No," quod the Catirpel. Alys therfore
To wayten nas not looth, for elles more
Was naught to do; she hoped, par aventure,   1015
Som worthi thyng to heren. In luxure
Hit sukked for som tym upon his spoon,
Then straughte his folded arms, oon aftyr oon,
And toke awei the spoon. "Thenchestow then,"
Quod hit, "that thou art chaunged?" "Ye! Often   1020
I shrynk or growe and thynges that I knewe
I can foryet." "What thynges?" "To saye trewe,"
Quod Alys sorwefully, "the Cukkow Songe
Gan faylen me, and came oute sadly wronge."
   "Reherse the *Lay*, then, *of the Grene Man.*"   1025
Alys folded hir handes and began:—

"Ye bene olde, Sir Bertilak," yonge Gawain seyde,   1026a
   "Tornen now whyte youre lokkes of grene,
But oft on youre hed ye stond wel apayde—
   Ought ye breech upward at youre age be sene?"

"Whan yonge, is long goon," Sir Berti answerede,   1026e
    "Methought of gret harm to my brayne,
Now certayn I have non I am not aferede
    To doon it agayne and agayne."

"Ye are olde," quod Sir Gawain, *"I tolde you bifore,*   1026i
    And youre middel is round as a vat,
But ye lepte up-so-doun as ye cam in the dore,
    Praye telle me how dyde ye do that?"

"When somwhat childgered," Sir Berti replied,   1026m
    "My mooder baked blancmange with pise,
She kept me deliver with pasties she fried—
    May I sell yow gode chepe som of thise?"

"Ye are olde, and lak cunning to carve up a bore,   1026q
    Yet at Yule at the dais I saw yow devour
King Arthurs hool serving on table and flore
    With bristles and tuskes and trotters all four!"

"Ech nyght in my bed I was let from my sleep   1026u
    As my ladye continued to speke,
And the discours she forced me to keep
    Muche strengthened my tethe and my cheke."

"Ye ben olde," sayde Sir Gawain, "a nik in your nek 1026y
    Myght knokke fro youre bulk youre round hed,
But stil with an eel on your nese ye can bek—   1026aa
    Of meschaunce then have ye no dred?"

"*Thryys I answerde your drasty grim speche*   1026cc
   That nought is," *quod Berti, "but ayre;*
Leste with myn axe I preve your last leche
   Fle hens ere I kicke you doun stayre!"   1026ff

"That is not sayde right," the Catirpel
Ajuged. "Not *al* was right, I knowe wel,"
Quod Alys humbly, "for som wordes fewe
Wer chaunged so I coude not speke hem trewe."   1030
   "Hit wrong is from biginninge unto end,"
With fors quod hit, "on that ye may depend;"
And in long silence dyde his croslet stir.
   The Catirpel spak first, and asked hir,
"What mesure wolde ye be?" "No fors, for chaunge,"   1035
Quod Alys hastyfly "to oft is straunge,

And weryyng, ye wot." "Nay, that I not,"
Quod hit. Alys sayde nought for anger hot,
So oft ne was she countrepleted never.
 "Be ye content?" "Nay, Sir, for I had lever   1040
A litel larger been, so plese yow.
Thre inches is a wrecched highte to grow."
 "Hit is a verray gode highte, certaynly!"
The Catirpel him heft up angrily
For hit was just thre inches high. But she   1045
In pitous voys of pletyng sayde, "For me
Hit nis my wone," and "I wissche," hir thought,
"The creatures so sone wrathed hem nought!"
 "In gode tyme shal ye find hit naturel,"
The Catirpel declared, "faire and wel."   1050
Into his mouth hit put the pyp and blew
As gold in croslet hit wolde maken new
And made the licour blubren in the pot.
 She wayted paciently until hit got
The spoon awei, and onys gaped or twyys   1055
And schoke hit self, and then descended ys
From of the musseroun and crept awei
Into the gras. "Oon side," she herde hit saye,
"Will cause yow grow, that oother shrynk." "Oon side
Of *what*?" she thought, and as hit had espyde   1060
Hir thought, "The musseroun," hit sayde, and lo!
Depe in the herbes was hit sone ygo.
 Syn hit was round, Alys at dulcarnoun
To fynde two sydes of the musseroun
Stode stil, but atte last hir arms she spred   1065
And brake two peces forthest fro hir hed.
 "Now which is which?" she sayde, and gan to tast
The right hand bit. Then whap! hir chin was fast
Agayn hir fot and she ner oute of wit,
So violent a strook she toke from hit.   1070

Forfrigted by this sodeyn chaunge, she knewe
She moot make hast, or shrynk awei lyk dewe.
Therfor that other pece she swiftly got
Ayenst hir mouth, but pressyng on hir fot
So hard hir chin was she myght hardly heve   1075
Apert hir lippes, but she dyde cheve
The taske at last. A morsel thanne she bit
Out of the lyft hand pece, and swalwed hit.

*   *   *   *
   *   *   *
*   *   *   *

"Aha!" cryde Alys in delite, "myn hed
Is free at last," but sone hir joy was fled   1080
By cause hir schuldres nawhit myght she se.
A merveillous long nek ros lyk a tre
From oute a se of leves binethe hir fer.
"What *is* that grene stoffe?" Alys sayde, "and wher,
Wher wentestow, my schuldres and my handes?"   1085
Mevyng hem litel dyde but in the landes
Binethe hir fer disturben gan the leves.
By cause they coude nat recche up fro the greves
To *hem* ward bent she doun hir hed, ful glad
A lithe and souple nek to fynde she had   1090
That lyk a serpent aiwher wolde bende.
In gracious arc hir swyre she dyde descende
In mynde to dive emong the leves that
Nobbut as though the forest wore an hat
The croppes wer of trees wherunder she   1095
Had wandered, when hissing at hir ee
A pigeon flew into her face and bete
Hir sharply with hir wynges in angir grete.
Alys drew swiftly bak. The Pigeon cried,

"Serpent!" and nolde not cese. Alys denied   1100
She nas no serpent: "Go, and lat me be!"
  "Serpent, I saye agayn," the Pigeon she
Repeted, softer though and terily,
"They nil not cese, how ernestly I try."
  "From hed to tayle I understond thee not,"   1105
Quod Alys. "Thou spekest tale of waltrot!"
  "Rotes of trees, and bonkes, hegges eke,"
The Pigeon sayde, maugre Alys cheke,
"I use, thise serpents nil nat ben apayde!"
  Alys woot lite of what this Pigeon sayde   1110
But thought hit wolde nat serve hir moore to speke
Til hit had made an ende. "Grete tene, so thee'k,"
The Pigeon sayde, "is hit to hacchen egges
But niht and daye I moot be of my legges
To been of serpents war! I myght nat slepe   1115
But thre hoole woukes tak of serpents kepe."
  "Hit peyneth me ye moot such noyaunce take,"
Quod Alys, now with cognisaunce awake.
  "I toke the highest tre withinne the wood,"
The Pigeon cryde, and shrighte as hit wer wood,   1120
"But whanne methought me fre of hem at last
Doun fro the welken wrythen they hem fast!
Ha, Serpent!" "*I* no serpent nam, by resoun
I make thee a protestacioun,"
Quod Alys, "for I am—I am—" "Ye, what   1125
Artow?" the Pigeon sayde. "I knowe that
Thou wilt som fals conceptioun set forth!"
  "A litel mayde am I," but south or north
So had she chaunged Alys coude nat se
How that hir wordes might bileved be.   1130
  "Ye, haselwode," the Pigeon sayde in scorn,
"Ful manie litel maydens that ben born
Myn ye hath seen, but noon had such a swyre.

A serpent thou, no smoke is without fire.
Thou wilt saye nexte thou never tasted egg!"   1135
    "I *have*," quod Alys soothfastly, "I beg
Thou understonde that litel maydes hem ete
As oft," quod she, "as serpents can hem frete!"
    "I leve hit not," the Pigeon sayde, "if so
Hit is, of serpent kinde I hold hem tho."   1140
    This straunge thought to Alys was so newe
Naught myght she say, wherfor in wordes fewe
"To seken egges soothly artow bent,"
The Pigeon sayde, "so mayden or serpent
I make no fors, thyn intent knowe I wel."   1145
    "What that I be concerneth *me* grete del,"
Alys replied hastyflye, "ne serche
I nat for egges; wolde I therat werche,
Syn rau I like hem not I nolde seke *thine*."
"With meschaunce, then," hit sourly sayde, "go dine!"   1150
And setled in hir nest. As wel she mow
Alys emong the trees coured low,
For with greet sleighte she most hir nek untie
That wrythed often in the braunches hie.
In tyme she gan remember that she helde   1155
Morsels of musseroun she yet coude welde
Which carfully on this syde first and then
On that she bit: schorter or longer when
She grewe she toke gode note, and sone she brought
Hir to hir propre highte as she so wrought.   1160
    Whan this was doon hir right mesure felt straunge,
So long it was syn she bigon to chaunge
But sone she used hit, and then bigan
To speken to hirself: "The half my plan,"
Quod she, "is doon. Forsooth I can not saye   1165
What I shal be, ech moment of the daye!
Nathles my highte is righte, now moot I go

Noot I not how, that swete gardyn into."
Than sodeynly she foond, within a stowe,
A litel hous som four fote high, or lowe.   1170
"Who liveth ther," she sayde, "if I sholde com
Upon hem large as this and fleme hem from
The place hir wittes will go wolleward!"
Bifore she wold aventure hir toward
The hous she nibbled at the right hand bit   1175
Til nine inch high she myght approchen hit.

CHAPITRE VI

Pig and Peper

Schorte while she stode and loked at the hous,
    Uncertayn what to do and daungerous,
When sodeynly, fot-hot from oute the wode
A fotman ran and at the dore he stode.   1180
(She juged him fotman for his liveree,
Though for his face a fissch she demed him be.)
So loude he knokked with his knokles sore
An oother fotman swiftly oped the dore,
In liveree also, and round of blee,   1185
With eyen large, and lyk a frogge was he;
Upon hir heddes crulled thikke they both
Had poudred haire. To listen nothing loth,
A litel from the wode crept Alys ner,
Ful curious to knowe hir chaffare ther.   1190
    The Fotman Fissch binethe his arm or fin
A lettre bore nigh large as he, and in
A voys solempne sayde, "Tak heere requeste
For Duchesse fro the Queen if pleye she leste
Pell-mell." The Fotman Frogge replied the same   1195

In voys solempne, but his wordes came
In ordre different, "Fro Queen requeste
For Duchesse to pley pell-mell an she leste."

    Then hed to hed they bowed, and hir haire
Togideres knotten gan hir crulles faire.   1200
    Alys therat so laughed that for ferde
They sholde hir heere bak to wode she ferde.
When nexte she peped oute the Fotman Fissch
Was gone; that oother Fotman sat foltisch
Upon the ground and kiked on the moon.   1205

She timorously to the dore gan goon
And knokked, but the Fotman Frogge sayde,
"Hit helpeth neveradel to knokke, yong mayde,
For resouns twayn: the first, that I am now
Upon the same side the dore as thow,   1210
And nexte, they maken on that oother side
So grete a noys that none myght heere, this tyde."
In feith a thonderous and myghty din
Of howling, nesing souned loude within,
With oft a crash as if som man a disshe   1215
Or ketel al to breken wolde wisshe.
    "Then plese yow," Alys sayde, "to tel me how
For me to intren is possiblë now."
    "Gode resoun wer to knokke," the Fotman sayde,
And merked nat the wordes of the mayde,   1220
"Suppos the dore betwix us stode, for then
Wertow withinne thou myghtest knokke, and when
Thou dydest I coude let thee faren oute."
He spak but sooth, of that she had no doute,
Uncurteisly, hit semed, for on high   1225
He loked while he spak, and not hir nigh.
"Per cas," hir thought, "he is constreyned thus,
And with his eyen nigh his top confus,
And yet he oghte answere what I pray
Which is," quod she, "how that I intren may."   1230
    "I shal sit here," the Fotman sayde, "until
Tomorwe—" long him thought that stede to fil,
But ope was flung the dore and from withinne
A platter flew that al but flayed the skinne
From of his nose, and breke upon a tre   1235
—"or nexte day, per cas, as we shal se,"
Continued the Fotman in no wise
Disturbled: hym the dische ne dyde supprise.

"How may I intren in?" in louder voys
Demanded Alys. "As for that, first choys   1240
Of questioun is, Shaltow com in at al?"
The Fotman sayde. "In feith, I hope I shal,"
Thought Alys soleinly. "Me liketh not
That al the creatures argue hot.
Hit is ynow to make a wight renne wode!"   1245
    The Fotman saw his chaunce and thought hit gode,
With wordes somdel newe, ageyn to say,
"I shal sit heere, now and then, fro day
To day for manie dayes." "But then what,"
Quod Alys, "doon moot I?" "Nay, as for that,   1250
As pleseth yow!" the Fotman sayde, and gan
To whistlen. Alys nigh despeired than:
"Hit boteth not to speken with a daf,"
Quod she, dyde ope the dore, and in she draf.

In right the dor in kicchen ful of smoke   1255
The Duchesse sat and at the fire a coke
Stirred a ketel stemyng ful of stewe.
    "To much of peper in the pot she strewe,"
Thought Alys, nesyng harde. And certaynly
To much of hit was in the ayre: strengly   1260
Nesed the Duchesse who a babee kepte
As on hir thre-leg stol she sat. Hit wepte
Houling and nesyng loude and nolde nat blinne.
Oonly the coke, outake a cat dyde grinne
From ere to ere and sat upon the herthe,   1265
Ne nesed nat. "Plese telle me why on erthe
Youre cat," sayde Alys somdel ferfully
Lest spekyng first she spak uncurteisly,
"Can grinnen as hit dooth?" The Duchesse sayde
"I merveille that thow nist not, litel mayde!   1270
For whi? Fro Chestre haileth hit. Thou Pig!"
    This laste word she spak so loude and big
That Alys sterted, til she saw she ment
Not Alys but the babee. On she went
Therfore: "Ne cunnen I that Chestre cats   1275
Grin ever, nor forsooth for strokes or pats
That ony can!" "Al can, and mostly do,"
The Duchesse sayde. "I knowe nat ony so,"
Sayde Alys curteislye, for to hir paye
Hit was, a parlement betwix hem tweye.   1280
    "Thou canst but lite, in sooth," the Duchesse sayde,
"Of cats or pigs, that may be wel assaid!"
    This lyked Alys not, and thought hit wel
Som oother theme to fynde on which to dwel.
But er she myght the coke the stewe toke   1285
From of the fire and gan in midst the smoke
Al she myght recchen at the Duchesse throw
And at the babee: iren toles now

From nigh the fire, then pannes, platters sone,
And dissches thikke at last cam manie one. 1290
The Duchesse made no fors though hire they hit,
And if the babee hurt when struck was hit
To say wer impossīblé, for algate
Hit houled long and loude. "Tak cure for that!"
Cryde Alys lepyng up and doun for fere. 1295
"Alas, his dere nose ye wol ofshere!"
Almost hit went: a bakyng pan flew past.
    "Sought every wight his owne chaffare, more fast
Sholde torn the nine speres in the ayre,"
The Duchesse grimly sayde. "The welken fayre 1300
Sholde litel gayn by that," quod Alys, proud
To show hir connyng, "hit sholde sterres croud
Doun fro hir spere, and Cytherea bring
With pestilence to Mars his mansionyng,
And what shal then bicom of us, I axe?" 1305
    "Hakke of hir hed, if ye minne me of an axe!"
The Duchesse sayde, and Alys fered lest
The coke that stirred stewe myght do hir hest,
But she to bisy was and listened not,
So Alys sayde, "The speres torn, I wot, 1310
In twelf or is hit four and twenty houres—"
    "I lerned never arsmetrike, in shoures
Dry or wet," the Duchesse sayde, "so pees!"
Than gan she nourisschen hir chylde, and ese
Hit lully lully with a song and shake 1315
So fiers his hed hit nei wat dyde oftake.

> *Speke grylly to your litel boy* 1316a
>   *And bete him wel for nesyng*
> *He doth hit oonly for anoy*
>   *And will do withoute cesyng.*

Than coke and babee tok hir part and sang
That in the rafters stif hir burdoun rang:

Ow! Ow! Ow!

1318a

The Duchesse while she sang the second vers
Hurled the babee up and doun so fers   1320
And violently the pore thyng houled so loude
To here the wordes Alys unnethe coude.

I speke ful grimly to my boy   1322a
Of purgatorye for nesyng
Him liketh peper, by Seinte Loy,
I say that withoute lesyng.

Burdoun
Ow! Ow! Ow!

1322e

"Thou mayst hit rokke, cacche hit if thou wilt,"
The Duchesse sayde, and flung hit, though hit spilt,
At Alys. "Now I most me redy make   1325
To pleyen pell-mell with the Quene." She spake,
And fot-hot lafte the roum. The coke as tyte
Threw after hir a pan, but dyde not hitte.
[How knewe she that the Quene had sent request
To pley pell-mell? The Fotman Frogge toke rest   1330
Withoute whan Alys ran to wode away:
Dyde he emong the fleynge pannes assay
To hand the lettre in the Fissch had brought
Ere Alys cam fro wode and entree sought?
Nay! Tyme and skille him fayled so to do;   1335
As in a dreme the lettre is ygo!]
With difficultee Alys caught and helde
The babee, whiche was straunge and kept stil selde.

His arms and legges poked nigh and fer
As if a ster-fissh, Alys thought, hit wer.   1340
Hit fnorteth lyk a whal, and eke hit bent
And straught up lyk a catirpel that went
In hast: unnethe myght Alys hold hit tight.
    Whan she had foond the way to hold hit right,
(Namely, to tye hit in a knotte, and gripe   1345
His right ere and left fot, how hard hit pipe,
That thus hit myght not stir, nor yet undo
Hitself), tyme was hir thought for hem to go.
She caried hit into the open ayre,
"Bi cause," quod she, "but I rescoue hit fayre,   1350
This chylde they shal withinne a day or twayn
Certaynly quelle! An if hit sholde remayn,
I seye, of mordre may I been acquit?"
She spak this laste word aloud, and hit
Gan grunten in replie (of nesyng had   1355
Hit doon ynow). "Forbere to grunt!" she bad,
"Hit is not right for thee to speken thus!"
    Agayn the babee grunted, as gotous,
And Alys loked in his face pertourbed
To see what hit so gretely had distourbed.   1360
His nose she saw was long and somdel stout
And lyk a swynes snute withouten dout,
His yes growinge much to smal to be
The yes of a naturel babee.
"This goth nat right," thought Alys, "but per cas   1365
Hit oonly sobbeth," but no tere ther nas.
    "If thou wilt tornen to a pig, my dere,"
Quod Alys ceriously, "I shal thee bere
No forther, be avysed!" The povre thyng
Sobbed agayn, or elles was gruntyng,   1370
She coude nat seyen which. They went on still,
And Alys wondred what of gode or ill

She myghte do with hit if she sholde bryng
Hit home, when sodeynly the litel thyng
Grunted so violently she was agast: 1375
No errour was, hit was a pig at last.

    To carie hit was folie, so she set
Hit doun to trot into the wode. "Go bet,"
Quod she, "for had hit grown hit wolde have been
Oon the ugliest chylde the world hath seen,   1380
But is a noble swyn." Tho gan she tell

Of chyldren that she knewe who
    wolde do well
As pigs if skil to chaunge hem wer,
    when lo!
The Chestre Cat supprised hir also,
For nigh hir in a tre on braunch
    hit satte,   1385
And grinned whan hit saw hir
    [which tre hatte
Aesculus hippocastanum by name,
Hors chasteyn tre in Englissh tung
    the same;

In Oxenford one in a garden grew,
A place that in hir playynge Alys knewe,   1390
And ther an auctor saw and smyled at
The chylde, who scheily spak to him.] The Cat
Semed to hir ful amyable yet,
But that his clawes wer long she nolde foryet,
And eke his manie teeth, therfor hir thought   1395
That wisdom wer honour she for hit wrought.

"Chestre Cat," timorously she bigan,
For fere hit lyked not the name, but whan
Hit oonly grinned wider glad was she:
"Thus fer hit semeth wel apayed to be," 1400
Hir thought, and bolder therby she went on,
"Sey prithee wher fro here wer best to gon?"
    "Dependeth," sayde the Cat, "to whiche stowe
Thou purposest to go." "I litel knowe
Or care of that—" quod she. "No fors what stigh," 1405
The Cat seyde, "thenne thou takest." "—com I nigh
Somwheres," Alys gan expoun. The Cat
Answerde therto, "Thou canst not fayle of that,
Walk thou but long ynow." This to deny
Alys ne coude, so "Sey me certaynly," 1410
A newe questioun she asked hit,
"What kind of people live here, I wolde wit?"
    "In *that* direccioun," answered the Cat,
"A Haberdashere woneth, and in *that*
A Merche Hare," rounde wavyng first his right 1415
And thanne his lyft paw aftyr. "Ye wel myght
As pleseth yow go visit ayther oon,
For both ben mad." "Ye? Nayther late ne soon
I nolde visit people that been mad."
    "No help for that," the Cat replied, "be glad, 1420
For we ar all mad here, both I and thow."
    "How wistow I am mad?" quod Alys, "how?"
    "Hit folweth, els thou noldest have com here."
    This preved not, thought Alys. "I wolde lere,"
Quod she, "how wistow thou art mad?" "A hound," 1425
The Cat sayde, "first, thou grantest for a pound,
Nis nat mad." "Yis," Alys sayde, "hit may be so."
    "Seestow nat then a hound wol grille him tho
With 'Gr-r-r' and wag his tayle when he is glad?
But I contrarious: thus am I mad." 1430

"But pr-r-r, not gr-r-r, I cal a cattes soun."
"To cal hit as thou lykest wer resoun,"
The Cat answered. "Shaltow pleye today
At pell-mell with the Queene?" "I wisshe I may,"
Quod Alys, "had I but request to go."   1435
    "There," quod the Cat, "shaltow me se," and so
Hit vanisshed. Supprised she was not,
So manie straunge happes as she wot,
But as she mused of his governaunce
So was she war his sodeyn apparaunce.   1440
    "What hap bifel the babee?" seyde the Cat,
"I nigh forgat to ask." "Why, as to that,"
Quod Alys stilly, as though naturally
Retorned had the Cat, "Unlustily,
Hit torned to a pig." "I thought hit sholde,"   1445
The Cat replied, and vanissht as hit wolde.
    She wayted if she myghte hit se ageyn,
But syn her wayting preved was in vayne,
She walked forth to wher the Merche Hare
Was seyde to wonen. "Haberdasheres yare   1450
I formerly have seen," she seyde, "by muche
The Merche Hare shal plese me more than suche.

Perchaunce hit shal not ben brayn wode in May
That now is, as in Merche hit was, in fay."
    She loked up, and sittyng on a braunch   1455
She saw the Cat ageyn, upon his haunch.
"Seydestow 'pig' or 'fige'?" quod the Cat.
    "I seyde 'pig'," quod Alys, "'swyn' is that.
Thy sodeyn vanisshyng and apparaunce
Let go, they make me gidi, with meschaunce!"   1460
    "Yis," quod the Cat, and vanisshed more slow,
From tayles ende until aloon dyde show
His grennyng, that remayned for som tyme
When al the rest was gone, both hed and lime.
    "Parfay," thought Alys, "often have I seen   1465
A cat that dyde not gren, but how may been
A grennyng sans a cat? So curiose
A thyng I never saw, as I suppose!"
    Not muchel forther cam bifore hir sight
The Merche Hares hous, the whiche was dight   1470
With chimneys shapen lyk a paire of eres
And thecched was the rof with furre and heres.
So large hit was she dorste not approche
Til she a peece of musseroun con broche
Lyft syde, and make hirself som two fot high.   1475
But somdel ferefully she cam hit nigh,
"I wisshe, wode mad suppos the Hare sholde be,
The Haberdashere I had gone to se!"

CHAPITRE VII

A Mad Reresouper Fest

Dight for a souper undernethe a tre
   A table dormaunt layde dyde Alys se,   1480
And ther the Merche Hare, bifore the hous,
And Haberdashere souped. A Dormous
On slepe betwix hem sat, the whiche they used
Lyk a whyssyne (hit nawhit refused)
To rest hir elbows on, and talk and gesse   1485
Abuf his hed. "This semeth confortlesse
And meschaunce for the Dormous," Alys thought,
"But slepyng doutelees hit careth nought."
    The table large was, but the thre con croude
Hem in an herne of hit. "No roum!" they loude   1490
Gan crye, "No roum!" as Alys drewe hem ner.
"*Plenté* of roum," she fersly cryde, "is ther!"
And in a chayr with armes, at one end
The table sat. "Haveth som wine, frend,"
The Merche Hare kindly sayde. Alys saw nought   1495

But ale, around the table though she sought.
"I se no wine," quod she. "Ther is none," sayde
The Merche Hare, and angrily the mayde
Replied, "Thenne hit nas nat courteous
To offren hit!" "Ne was to sit with us   1500
Withouten oure request!" the Merche Hare sayde.
"I noot hit was *youre* table, hit is layde
For manie moore than thre!" "Thyn haire hath nede,"
The Haberdashere sayde, "of kittyng!" Hede
Of Alys with grete curiositee   1505
He had for som tyme taken, ere that he
This firste speche wolde proferen. "Parfey,
Thou owest lerne," gan Alys sternly sey,
"That sawes personeles to usen nis
Not hende: contrarie to honour hit is!"   1510

The Haberdashere oped yes wyde
Whanne he herde this but oonly *sayde,* that tyde,
"Why is a hrafen lyk a scribes deske?"
"Now here is game," thought Alys, "for to eske
Hem ridels I am glad they have bigoon—   1515
I leve," she sayde aloude to him, "that oon
I coude gesse, iwis." "Menestow that
Thou thenchest thou canst fynde the answere plat?"
The Merche Hare sayde. "Just so," quod Alys, "yis."
"Thou owest sey then as thy menyng is,"   1520
The Merche Hare sayde. "I do, for what I sey
I mene,"quod Alys, "that is, par ma fay,
I mene what I seye, no difference is."
"Forsooth," the Haberdashere sayde, "that nis
The same. For equally thou myghtest say   1525
'I se al that I ete' ne differ may
Fro that 'I ete al that I se.'" The Hare
Addicion made, "Thou myghtest ben unware
'I lyk what that I get' nis not the same
As 'What I lyk I get.' The Dormous came   1530
Though semyng stil on slepe, with "Just as wel
To seye 'I brethe whan that I slepe' wol tel
No different from 'I slepe whan that I brethe.'"
"With thee," the Haberdashere sayde, "unnethe
May oon the difference fynde!" No more they spak   1535
While Alys thought of al she myght cal bak
Of hrafens and of scribes deskes, whiche nas
But litel, til the Haberdashere was
The first to speke. "What day of month is hit?"
He asked Alys. Frouning he dyde sit   1540
And loked on his chylindre, whiche he
Wayved to catch the sunnes light, a tre
Preventyng hit. Alys considered,
And seyde, "The fourth." "Two dayes, by my hed,"—

[The thridde of May was Chaucers choysest date: 1545
Alys went doun the douvre one day late!]—
The Haberdashere siked, "is hit wrong.
I told thee butre sholde not make hit strong!"
He loked angrily upon the Hare.
　　"It was the *beste* butre we coude spare,"   1550
The Merche Hare replied. "Morsels of breed
Cam of thi knyff. Hit was a foly deed
To use thi trenchur knyff to smere hit on!
Hit letteth al the light that on hit shon!"
The Haberdashere seyde. The Hare toke   1555
The chylindre and dismally dyde loke
At hit, and plounged hit into his ale,
But nought coude seye, outtake, with face pale,
His former sawe, "Hit was the *beste* buttre!"
　　Alys was lokyng at hit past his shuldre: 1560
"A silly chylindre hit semeth me,"
She seyde, "hit telleth what the daye sholde be,
But not the hour!" "Ye, what importeth that?"
The Haberdashere muttred as he sat.
"Telleth your chylindre what yere hit is?"   1565
"Certaynly not," redily sayde Alys,
"Bi cause the yere remayneth without chaunge
So long togider that hit nis not straunge."
　　"Mine doth the same," the Haberdashere sayde.
The *matiere* was Englyssh, but conveyde   1570
No *sen* to Alys, so she courtaysly
Replied, "I understonde thee not, pardy!"
　　"In feith, the Dormous is on slepe ageyn."
The Haberdashere let a litel rain
Of hoote spiced ale pouren on   1575
His nose. The Dormous schoke his hed anon
And sayde, but oped not his yes, "Sooth
Forsooth, that wolde I seye, upon mine ooth!"

The Haberdashere asked Alys tho
"Hastow yet gesst the ridel?" She seyde, "No.   1580
I let hit goo! Sey what the answer is."
"I woot namoore than sparwes on a ris!"
"Nor I," the Hare seyde. Werily
She siked. "Ye myght doon more honestly
With tyme than wasting hit with ridels that   1585
Are answerlees, I rekene, by my hat!"
[If lak of answer maketh irous thought,
One answer is, if answer most be sought:
A hrafen hath a bille and manie quilles
A scribes deske a quille and manie billes!]   1590
    The Haberdashere seyde, "If thou knewe Tyme
As wel as I, ye wol nat speke of *him*
As wastyng '*hit*'." "I noot what menestow,
Nor how in mynde of tyme demestow,"
Quod she. "No wonder is, for I suppose,"   1595
He seyde, and scornfully lifte up his nose,
"Thou never even spak to Tyme!" "Per cas
I dyde not," Alys cautelously, as
Hire semed wise, replied. "But yet I knowe
That I most beten tyme hie and lowe   1600
When I lerne musike." "A, then that is why,"
The Haberdashere seyde, "for never nilly
Enduren betyng. But, freonden him,
And he wol do your bidding with the tyme
Upon the klokke. *Exempli gratia*,   1605
Suppos thou soughtest leiser, *otia*,
At prime, when lessouns sholde been beginninge,
Whisper to Tyme, and in a twinkelinge
Prime shal be noon, and diner tyme!" ("I wisshe,"
The Hare sayde, "diner were here in a disshe!")   1610
    "Bettre than wel," sayde Alys thoughtfully,
"But then, thou wist, I nolde been hungri."

The Haberdashere seyde, "At fyrst, perchaunce,
But then thou coudest let not tyme avaunce
Past noon!" "Is that," quod she, "*thi* maner werk?"   1615
He nikked sadly nay. "A querele sterk
In Merche we had, ere *he* went mad, thou wist"
(He poked with a spoon he held in fist
Towards the Hare), "when at a minstrelcye
Bifore the Quene of Hertes merrilye   1620
Hit fell to me to sing 'An hendy hap'
That telleth how I caught a sodeyn rap:

An hendy hap on me was sent   1622a
From skyes lyk a thonder dent

Hast herde the song, perchaunce?" "Oon somwhat lyk,"
Seyde Alys. "Thus the woordes nexte forth strike:

> *My wittes all from me is went*   1624a
> *A rof-tile strook my croun.*
>   *An hendy hap—"*   1624c

The Dormous schoke hitself, and in his slepe   1625
"An hendy hap" the song bigan to kepe
"An *hendy, hendy, hendy hap hap hap*"
So long hit sang his hed they moste flap
To make hit stop. "I scarsly myght conclude
The first vers, when the Quene, in loude voys rude,"   1630
The Haberdashere seyd, "yeyed, irous red,
'He mordereth the tyme! Of with his hed!'"
    "How ferfully sauvage!" cryde Alys tho.
    "Sythen," he made countenaunce of wo,
"He nil doon naught I aske. The tyme of daye   1635
Stant ever even, souper tyme, parfaye."
[Oonly the daye his chylindre nede merk,
Therfore, not houres dawenyng til derk.]
    Thanne sodeynly gan Alys comprehende
A thyng: "Is that the resoun, or the ende,   1640
For which the table bereth so much stuff?"
    "Hit is," the Haberdashere siked, "huff!
Ever is souper tyme, no Tyme have we
To wassh the vessels that we se
Been used." "Round the table douteles   1645
Ye meven, then?" seyde Alys. Quod he, "Yes.
We use the thynges and meve on to newe."
    "What happeth when ye moste beginne anewe?"
But for this ridel was noon answer founde.
    "Suppos we chese another theme this stounde,"   1650
The Merche Hare gaping seyde. "This werieth me.

I pose the yong mayde telle a tale." Quod she
In hast, afright, "Ne can I noon, alas!"
   "Than shal the Dormous give us that solas,"
They cryed both. "Dormous, awak!" and so   1655
On bothe sydes pincched they hit tho.
The Dormous slowly opened his yes
And loked blerily, and gaped thries.
"I nas on slepe," hit seyde feblely,
"Ech woord ye spak I herde certaynly."   1660
   "Telle us a tale!" the Hare seyde him to.
"Ye, an thou wilt, I preye thee, Dormous, do!"
Cryde Alys egrely. "Begin as tyte,"
The Haberdashere seyde, "or wel we wit
That thou wilt slepe before hit recheth fin."   1665
   In grete hast the Dormous dyde begin,
"In arre dawes, as thise stories sey,
Of Ector, Charlemagne and Arthour fey,
Thre litel sostres, namely Marie,
Matilda, Helen, woned tidily   1670
Togeder at the bottom of a well—"
   "What lyflode had they ther wher they dyde dwell?"
Quod Alys, ever fayn of mete and drynk
To here. The Dormous most a while thynk.
At laste hit seyde, "Hir lyflode was triacle."   1675
   "Nay, they sholde have caught a cardynacle,"
Gentilly she seyde. "They sholde been seke."
   "Wel hool they were, an ye of poysoun speke!"
Alys in hir ymaginacioun
Coude not conceyve of what complexioun   1680
So straunge a lyf most be. "Why dyde they dwelle,"
She asked, "at the bottom of a welle?"
   Ful ernestly the Merche Hare bade hir, "Tak
Of this moyst ale som more, and have no lak."
   "Naught have I had," she seyde, and made hit tough,

"And therfore can I not tak moore." "Ynough!"   1686
The Haberdashere seyde, "Thou menest lesse
Thou canst not take. Ful esy, mayst thou gesse,
Hit is to taken more than naught." "No man
Requireth *your* opinion," quod she than.   1690
 "Who maketh sawes personeles now?"
The Haberdashere gladly cryde, "Thow!"
 Niste Alys not a word to seye to this,
So toke som breed and ale hirself, ywis,
And tornyng to the Dormous seyde ageyn,   1695
"Why dwelt they in a well, I aske thee pleyn?"
 After long thought the Dormous gan expoun,
"Triacle welle hit was." "An ill resoun!
Ther nis not such a thyng," ful angrily
Alys bigan, but "Hush! Hush!" gentilly   1700
The Hare and Haberdashere snybbed hir.
The gloomy Dormous wolde no forther stir,
But "If," hit seyde, "thou canst no cortayse
Thou mayst tell on the tale to end for me."
 "No, praye continue," Alys humbly seyde,   1705
"To entremette ageyn my tong is stayde.
Sans doute ther may be *oon*!" "What, oon oonly?"
The Dormous answerde somdel wrathfully,
But natheles to telle on dyde agree.
"They lerne to drawe, thise litel sostres thre—"   1710
"What dyde they drawe?" quod Alys, who foryat
What she had promised. "Triacle," flat
The Dormous seyde, withoute consideryng.
 Tho seyde the Haberdashere, entremettyng,
"I lak a clene coppe, one place meve we on!"   1715
He meved as he spake, and therupon
The Dormous folwed him, whose place the Hare
Then toke, and Alys with unwilling care
Sat in the Hares sete. Non avauntage

Got eny save the Haberdashere sage;   1720
For Alys was hit wers, for in his platter
The Hare had newly torned the ale pot over.
     Alys, for fere she myght ageyn offende
The Dormous, carefully dyde hir commende.
"I understonde thee not. Triacle whens   1725
I preye thee myght they drawe?" "Hadst thou but sens,"
The Haberdashere seyde, "thou coudest minne
Water is drawn from wells with water inne,
So lykwise triacle from welles wher
Triacle is, not so, cukkow?" "They wer   1730
Fast in the welle," seyde she, and made no fors
Of what he seyde, hit harmed not hir cors.
"Bi course they wer," the Dormous seyde, "welle in."
     This semed unto Alys resoun thin,
But so confus by this she was she let   1735
The Dormous speke on for a while as yet.
     "Lernyng to drawe they drewe," hit gan to seyen
Gaping for slepe and rubbing at his eyen,
"All maner of thynges that bigan with M—"
"Whi with an M?" The Merche Hare seyde "Ahem!   1740
Whi not?" Naught Alys sayde. Nei wat on slepe
The Dormous gan his yes shutte to kepe
But pincched by the Haberdashere wook
And with a litel shrike anon forth strook,
"—that with an M beginne, mous-falles, moon,   1745
Memorie, mucheness—for, night or noon,
Ye here of incres drawinge to a muchnesse,
That is, when thynges grow to grete from lesse.
A drawinge of a muchnesse hastow seen?"
     "Forsooth, now that required have I been,"   1750
Quod she, confus, "I cannot thenche—" "Then cese
Of talkyng," seyde the Haberdashere. "Pese!"
So rude was this that Alys ros and went

In grete displesaunce. The Dormous glent
On slepe at onys, and that other twayn   1755
Ne noted not that she was gone, though fayn
She wolde here hem call to hir, and twyis
She loked bak. The laste tyme Alys
Had sighte of hem, into the ale pot they
Had sought to croud the Dormous, ther to stay.   1760

"Algate," quod Alys, mevyng through the wode,
"Visiten *ther* ageyn, though I wer wode,
I never nil! So foltisch, ful of stryf,
A souper never saw I in my lyf!"

As thus she spoke she saw within a tree   1765
A dore that led directly in. Quod she,
"Ful coryouse, lyk everythyng today!
Methynketh I myght intren, par ma fay!"
And in she went. Ageyn she found she was
Within the long hall nigh the table glas.   1770
"This tyme," she toold hirself, "I shal do right,"
And first she toke the gylden keye, and pight
Hit in the lokke to ope the gardyn dore,
Then set to werk to nibblen lesse or more
Of musseroun she kepte withinne hir sak,   1775
Til of a fote in highte she lite dyde lak.
Then doun the litel passage walked she,
And *then*—she foond hirsel wher she wolde be,
Within the lufly gardyn now at last,
Emang briht floures and cool founteyns fast.   1780

The Quenes Pell-Mell Ground

Nigh to the dore, within the gardyn grew
 A roser large, with roses white on hewe,
The which thre gardineres bisily
Were peinting red. Alys curiously
Drew ner, to wacchen how they myghte thrive,   1785
And oon of hem herde crye, "Be war now, Five,
Forbere to sprengen me with peint so muche!"
 "That myght I not avoiden," Five gan grucche,
"For hit was Seven jogged min elbow."
 Seven glent up and seyde, "Ryght dost thow,   1790
Five, that ever on othres puttest blame!"
 "For *thee* silence is best," seyde Five, "for shame!
But yisterday I herde the Quene sey
Bihoveth thee bihedding, is no nay."
 "What had he doon?" enquered egrely   1795
The first that spake. Cryde Seven angrily,
"Pees, Two! For nought is that thy besiship."

"His besiship hit is, in felawship,"
Quod Five, "and I shal telle him how hit was—
He brought unto the cook, with sory gras,   1800
Wortes in stede of onions." Seven flang
His brusch on ground, "Unriht hit is and wrang,"
He gan to seye, when, at aventure
He Alys seigh with ye, wher she, unsure,
Stode wacching hem. He chekked sodeynly,   1805
And with the othres bowed worthshiply.

"Whi peinten ye thise roses, telleth me,
I preye yow," somdel ferefully quod she.

Seven and Five seyde naught, but glent on Two,
As they wolde he made answer to hir tho.   1810
In lowe voys Two bigan, "Maistresse,
In sooth, thou wist, this roser that we dresse
Oweth to have been red, but bi meschaunce
We put a white oon in, and wit perchaunce
The Quene therof, we all shal hadet be.   1815
Therfore bifore she come attempten we—"
But right then Five, the gardyn serchyng round,
Gan crye, "The Quene, the Quene!" and on the ground
As tyte fell gruf the gardineres thre.
       At soun of manie marchyng feet, to se   1820
The Quene gan Alys tornen egrely:
First cam ten soudeurs that dyde clubbes carie,
In shape lyk the thre, oblong and flat,
Hir feet and handes at the angels sat.
Nexte cam ten curteours, anorned alle   1825
With diamants, and lyk the soudeurs talle
Walkt two and two. Theraftyr hand in hand
The royal children, ten wer in hir band,
In couples daunced merrily along;
Anornd with hertes was this joly throng.   1830
Nexte cam the gestes, Quenes with hir Kinge
Most were, and hem emang the White Coninge.
Hit talked hastyflye and ferefully,
Smilyng at alle they seyde, and trotted by
Not noting hir. Behind hem cam the Knave   1835
Of Hertes dresst, that on a whyssyne brave
Of cremesin velvet brought the Kinges croun,
And last of alle this grand processioun
Came by THE KING OF HERTES AND THE QUENE.
       Unsure was Alys wher she sholde bidene   1840
Lie grovellyng as dyde ech gardiner
Biside his newly peinted red roser,

But in hir mynd was no rememberaunce
Of such a rewle. "Moreover, if per chaunce
Processiouns sholde pass, what gode were hit 1845
If alle moot on hir faces lie as tyte,"
Hir thought, "so they no part therof myght se?"
She stode therfore in place, ther wayted she.
    Whan the processioun cam opposite
To hir, they stopped alle, as they wolde wit 1850
Hir besines there, and sternely spak the Quene,
"Who may this be?" She asked, for his tene,
The Knave of Hertes, that coude oonly bow
And smile. "Idiote," quod the Quene, "I vow!"
She schok hir hed impaciently, and seyde 1855
Tornyng to Alys, "Seye thi name, mayde!"
    "My name is Alys, if so plese the,"
Seyde Alys cortaysly, "thi Mageste."
But to hirself she seyde, "What may bifalle?
Nought but a pakke of cardes been they alle! 1860
Me nedeth not to quake for fere of hem."
    "And who been *thise,* that by the roser stem
Upon hir faces lie?" seyde thanne the Quene,
For as hir peintures myghte not be sene,
And as the patron drawn upon hir bak 1865
The same was as the othres of the pak,
She wiste not wher they gardineres wer
Or curteours or soudeurs that laye ther,
Or of hir owene children thre, perchaunce.
    "How sholde *I* wit? Fro here and into Fraunce," 1870
Quod Alys, supprised bi hir corage,
"No besinesse is hit of *mine*!" In rage
The Quene torned cremison in rode;
With yes glaringe lyk a best she stode,
And gan to shrike, "Of with hir hed! Of with—" 1875
    "Folie!" seyde Alys, "waltrot is, long sith."

The Quene coude no moore seye, and on hir arm
The King layde gentilly his hand. "Noon harm,"
He seyde, "she ment, for but a chylde she is."

The Quene torned angrily awei at this   1880
Fro him, and "Torn hem over!" bade the Knave.
With an fot dyde the Knave hem over have.
    "Stondeth ye!" shrilly and loude cryde the Quene.
Thanne stode the gardineres thre bidene
And bowen gan to King, to Quene, to alle   1885

Around, and to the children eke roialle.
"Beth stille!" she scremed, "ye make me toti thus!
Your roser werke now tyme is to discuss."
"So plese thi Mageste," seyde Two humblye,
And kneled on his knee, "attemprelye—"   1890
The Quene gan examinen the tre.
"*I* se. Of with hir heds!" commaunded she.
Whan meven gan the hoole processioun
Thre soudeurs for the execucioun
Bilef. To Alys to defende hem than   1895
The thre unhapi gardineres ran.
"Hadet ye shal not be!" cryde Alys, and
Into a pot of floures nigh at hand
She cointly put hem. Litel diligence
To serchen had the soudeurs thre: sone thence   1900
They marched aftyr othres in the pak;
No boot was ther to stay or loken bak.
Schouted the Quene, "Ben hir heddes of?"
"Hir heds ben gone," replied the soudeurs cof,
"So plese thi Mageste." "Right doon have ye,"   1905
Schouted the Quene. "Canstow pley with me
Pell-mell?" The soudeurs answered naught, but glent
On Alys, for the questioun was ment
Sans doute for hir. "Yis!" schouted Alys. "Thanne
Come on!" rored the Quene, and Alys gan   1910
Joinen the othres in processioun
And wondered much in what condicioun
The Wheel of Fortune sholde torn. A voys
Biside hir, somdel fereful and courtois,
"This is—" hit seyde, "this is a clere bright day!"   1915
It was the White Coninge, *si'l vous plait*,
That pired ferefully into hir face.
"Ye," quod she. "Is the Duchesse in this place?"
"Husch!" seyde the Coninge, low and hastyfly.

He glent behind his schuldre ferefully,   1920
Stode on his toos and whispered in hir ere,
"Hir sentence is for execucion here!"
        "Whi?"Alys seyde. "Dydst thou sey, 'Alas!'?"
The Coninge asked. "Nay, with sory grace,
Of that no fors!" quod Alys. "I seyde 'Whi?'"   1925
        "A box, a bobet on the eres hi
She gaf the Quene—" the Coninge bigan.
A screme of lahter Alys utred than.
"A, husch!" the Coninge whispered, afrayd,
"The Quene shal here the! Understonde, she seyde   1930
Bi cause the Duchesse somdel late was sene—"
        "Goth to youre stedes!" thondered the Quene,
And to and fro gan people runnen tyte
And tomblyng an ageynst another hit
But setled sone and than began the game.   1935
        The Quenes pell-mell ground to which they came
Was coryouse as ever Alys sawe,
With rigges and with forwes in rogh rawe;
The pell-mell balles hurchouns wer on live,
The maillets swanes, and the soudeurs five   1940
Or more bent doun on handes and on fet
To serve as arches. Alys coude not hete
Hir swan to serve hir right, for whan she had
His cors binethe hir arm in confort stad,
With legges hanginge doun, and swyre oute straughte,   1945
And with his hed the irchon wolde have raughte,
Hit *wolde* twisten round and suche a look
Into hir face of wonderyng hit took
She moste laughe oute loude. Than whan his hals
Was straught ageyn, the irchon pleyed fals,   1950
Hitself uncrulled, and wolde crepe awei.
Oft stode a forwe or a rigge in wei
Wher Alys wolde send the irchon to;

The soudeurs bending heds doun to hir sho
Continually stode uppe, and walked of   1955
To othre ground. Alys concluded cof
The game biset was with grete difficultee.

The pleyers alle ne pleyed not by degree
But with muche stryf, and for the irchons fought.
Ful sone the Quene, wood wrathe to furie wrought,   1960
Gan stampe about, and schout, "Of with his hed!"
Or elles "with hir hed," ech minute dred.

Alys gan fere, although as yet resoun
Was noon, for she no disputacioun
Had with the Quene, but sone hit myght so hap,   1965
"And then," she thought, "I sholde receyve a rap!
Such lust they have for heddyng people here
Grete wonder is ought livyng doth appere!"
    She serched round to se if she coude scape
And myght departe unseen. A coryouse shape   1970
She wondred at appered in the ayre:
Wacchyng she found hit was a grennung faire,
And seyde, "The Chestre Cat hit is, now gayne
I shal a freend to talken with ageyn."
    "How spedest thou?" the Cat bigan forthwith   1975
Whan mouthe ynow hit had to speken with.
She wayted til the eyen came, and gave
A nod, for no use was to speken, save
Whan eres came, or atte leste one.
The Cattes hoole hed appered sone,   1980
And Alys put her swanne doun, and toold
Hir tale as touchyng on the game, ful boold
And glad she coude speke to eni wight.
The Cat ajuged that, with hed in sight,
Ynough of Cat for conversacion   1985
Appered had: of more there neded non.
    "I thenche not they pleye with justice tho,"
Compleyned Alys, "and they querele so
I may not here me speke, and lawes none
They seem to have, or an they do they done   1990
No fors of hem, nor canstow thenche what tene
Hit is the thynges ben alle quicke, I mene,
The arch wherthrough I sholde my irchon send
Walketh now fer and wol not for me bend,
And whan I sholde the Quenes irchon hit   1995
With blow of mine ful swift awei ran hit!"

"How liketh yow the Quene?" asked the Cat
In softe voys and lowe. "A fig for that!"
Quod Alys, "she is so excessively—"
She noted that the Quene intentyfly   2000
Bihind hir listened, so seyde, "—lik to win
Hit helpeth lite to bryng the game to fin."
Therat the Quene smilyng paced on.
    "Whom spekest thou unto, I wille con?"
The King to Alys seyde, and wondered   2005
On lokyng at the Chestre Cattes hed.
    "Hit is my friend, a Chestre Cat, lat me
Acqueynte yow, this is hit, and this is he."
    "No whit me liketh hit," the King gan seye
"But if hit wille kiss min hand, hit maye."   2010
    "I nil," the Cat seyde. "What? Show reverence,
Ne look on me with grim persèverance,"
Enjoined the King, but hid him as he spak
Bihinden Alys, stondynge at hir bak.
    "A cat," quod Alys, "may look at a king,   2015
Though noot I in what bok I rede that thyng."
    "Nathles, withouten disputicioun
Hit most be meued, taken out of toun,"
Determined the King, and to the Quene
He seyde, "My dere, I wissh this cat bidene   2020
Wer meued." Of every difficultee
She had one oonly sovereyne remedee.
"Of with his hed!" she seyde, and tok no keep
Even to torn hir own. "I shal not sleep
Til I have brought the baser," cryde the King,   2025
And ran of egrely an axe to bring.
    Alys determined to go bak and se
How went the game, for in the distance she
Myght here the Quene with furie screme, and pass
Sentence on pleyers thre with sory gras   2030

For they had misst hir tornes. Thynges thus
At yfel stode; the game was so confus
She niste wher hit was hir torn or no.
Therfor to seke hir irchon went she tho.
    The irchon with an othre irchon fought,   2035
So Alys an on othre striken thought,
Accordaunt to the lawes of the game,
But now hir maillet swan, she saw with grame,
Was gone, and wolde flien, an hit myght,
Into a tre that fer of was in sight.   2040
    Whan she had caught and brought hit bak, she found,
The fecht ydoon, the irchons lafte the ground.
"No fors," she seyde, "the arches beyng gone,"
And held the swan bineth hir arm that sone
Hit myght not scape, and went to seke hir freend.   2045
    Around the Chestre Cat she foond, at end,
Supprisyngly, were crouded manie oon.
In proces was a disputacion
Betwene the execucioner, the King
And Quene, who talked without listenyng,   2050
While alle the rest in silence wacched grim
And litel confort drewe fro hir or him.
As sone as Alys cam, apelin gan
Alle thre to hir, hir arguments bigan
Ageyn to hir, and alle togider spoke   2055
That she unnethe hir menyng undertoke.
    The execucioneres argument
Was that to cut a hed of nedes ment
A cors most be, to cut the hed of fro,
No precedent in lyf had he and so   2060
Wolde nat beginne now his age was such.
    The Kinges argument was just this much:
What had a hed myght heded be, no use
To speken folie or the dede refuse.

The Quenes argument was that if naught   2065
Wer doon as tyte and tyter, alle who aught
A hed aiwher she wolde hem execute.
(This was hit made hem alle aferde and mute.)
    Alys coude oonly seye, "Unto the Duchesse
This Cat bilongeth, aske ye hir, I gesse."   2070
    "She is in prisoun, fecche hir here," the Quene
Demanded, and the baser ran bidene.
    Whan he was gone the Cattes hed grew fade
And feint, and whan he brought the Duchesse, had
Evanisshed and gone, and so the King   2075
And execucioner ran wildly lokyng
Up and doun for hit, while alle the rest
Retorned to the game, as hem thought best.

The Mokke Se-Tortuses Tale

"Ye may not thenche," quod she, "my derest fere,
   How glad ageyn I am to se yow here!"   2080
The Duchesse lufly into Alys arm
Hir elbow crucken gan, and dyde no harm
As walked they awei togider. Glad
Was Alys that the Duchesse, who so bad
Had semed in the kicchene when they met,   2085
So plesaunte was, hir former ire foryet.
Oonly the peper made hir fiers, perchaunce.
    "Whan *I* a Duchesse am, as hit may chaunce,"
Hir thought (though litel hope therof she hadde),
"No peper shal, to maken people madde,   2090
Be stored in my kicchene, noon *at al*—
The coke and kicchene wenche inform I shal,
The stewe hit nedeth not. Peper, I wot,
Maketh man algate colerik and hot."
This newe reule to fynde, hir thought hit skile.   2095

"Vinegre maketh sour, and camomille
Man maketh bittre—sucre, spicerie,
Daintees, and cakes baked with honie
Make children swete: knewe people *that,* I wene,
So nigardlye of such they nolde bene."   2100

By this she had the Duchesse ful foryete,
And lept whan nigh hir ere a voys hir gret.

"My dere, thou thenchest of som thyng, and so
Foryete to talke. What moral comth ther fro
As yet I cannot seye, but in schort tyme   2105
I shal remembre hit, in prose or rime."
    "Per cas it hath none,"Alys seyde boold.
    "Nay, childe, nay," the Duchesse seyde, "I hoold
Alle thyng hath a moral, canstow hit fynde,"
And ner to Alys threst hirself unkynde.   2110
    Ne liked Alys that she came so nigh,
So *fully* foule was she, and just so high
She was she myght on Alys shuldre rest
Hir chin that scharpe was lyk a pin. As best
She myght she bar hit, oute of cortaysé.   2115
    Somwhat to seye, "The game now goth," quod she,
"Bettre than erst." "Hit doth," the Duchesse seyde,
"Wherof the moral is, when wel assaid,
'Is love, is love, wol torn the speres nine!'"
    "One seyde," she whispered, "in eres mine,   2120
Hit limpeth whan that every wight wol seke
His owne chaffare!" "In feith, hit dooth, so thee'k!"
The Duchesse seyde, and delved depe and sore
Hir scharpe smal chin in Alys shuldre more,
"That meneth much the same. And take gode keep,   2125
Sans doute the moral *therof* is that 'sleep
The norice of digestioun is,' and eke
'Is ydelnesse'—now herken what I speke—
'The ministre and the norice unto vices'
That comen from indulgence in delices."   2130
    "How muche hit liketh hir fro alle thyng,"
Thought Alys, "som newe moral oute to bryng!"
    "Per cas," the Duchesse seyde, "thou wondyrest
"Whi put I not my arm aboute thi west.
The resoun is I doute how irous may   2135
Thi swan bicom. Nathles shal I assay?"

"He mighte bite," seyde Alys carefully,
Th'assai she nolde awayten egrely.
"Forsooth," the Duchesse seyde, "mustarde and swan
Wol bothe bite, whence we the moral can   2140
'Briddes of kinde togider flye.'" "Mustarde,"
Quod Alys, "nis a brid." "So have I harde.
Thou'rt right," the Duchesse seyde, "so clerely put!"
    "A mineral hit is, as men repute,"
Seyde Alys, though unsure. "In feith, hit is,"   2145
The Duchesse seyde, who wolde in that or this
That Alys seyde agree: "nigh stondeth here
A mustarde engin large. The moral there
Is 'Have I more, the lasse is lafte for thee.'"
    "I knowe!" cryde Alys, for noon heed toke she   2150
Of this last sawe, "hit is an herbe, I wene,
Al semeth hit not so." "So do I mene,"
The Duchesse seyde, "of that the moral is
'Be as thou woldest seme,' or sholde I this
More simply seye, 'Thenche not thiself to be   2155
Not othre than myghte othres thenche to se
That what thou wert or myght be diffred not
From what thou hadst ben wolde have let hem wot
Hit nis not othre wise." "The bettre myght
I understonde hit wer hit writ doun right,"   2160
Quod Alys cortaysely, "but whan ye seye
The matter, goth the sense from me aweye."
    "I coude more seye than that if I sholde chese,"
She seyde, for Alys woordes dyde hir plese.
    "I praye thou noldest trublen thee to saye   2165
Hit lenger than this," quod Alys. "Dismaye
Thee not ne talk of truble! Taketh alle
That I have seyde as yet as yifte I shal
Thee give." "Gode chepe that yifte!" thought Alys, glad
Such yiftes not on holy days wer had.   2170

But this for fer of ire she nolde saye
Aloude. "What, thenchestow ageyn, I praye?"
The Duchesse seyde, and dug hir scharpe chin
With painful thrust in Alys shuldre in.
"My right hit is to thenche," seyde scharply she,   2175
A litel trubled. "Ner as much as be
A pigges right to flye, wherof the m—"
    Alys had wondyr that hir voys gan stem
Even in midst hir favored woord 'moral',
And tremblen gan the arm that linked al   2180
In Alys was. Alys loked up. Ther stode
The Quene bifore hem, frounyng, fiers in mode,
With folded arms, blak browed lyk the sky
Whan thonder dint wol fal and windes fly.
    "Bright daye, your Mageste," in feble voys   2185
The Duchesse seyde. "Be war, and take thi choys,"
Shouted the Quene, and smoot hir fot on ground,
"Thou or thy hed moot of and not be found
In half no tyme!" The Duchesse toke hir choys,
And went as tyte, sans moral and sans noise.   2190
    "Lat us continewe with the game," the Quene
Bede Alys, who for fere ne durst not mene
To seye a word, but slowly at hir bak
Retorned to the court, wher gestes slak
In schade while absent was the Quene toke rest   2195
Til they hir seigh, when hastyflye as best
They myght they ran, for ony smal delay
Sholde cost hir lives, if they forbore to play.
    Thurghout the game the Quene kept quarrelyng
With al the othre pleyers, and shoutyng   2200
"Of with his hed," or "with hir hed!" Than must
The soudeurs those she demde in prisoun thrust
And cese to bend as arches, so that sone
In al the pell-mell ground was lafte there none,

The pleyers waytyng execucioun,   2205
Save King and Quene and Alys, in prisoun.
    Then brethles cesed of hir ire the Quene.
"Hastow as yet the Mokke Se-Tortus sene?"
She asked Alys. "Nay. I noot what is
A Mokke Tortus." "Se-tortus, ywis: 2210
The thyng mokke tortus stewe is coked from."
    "Such saw ne herde I never, blinde or dom."
    "Than come," the Quene seyde, "and his historye
He shal the telle." To all the companye
As they went of dyde Alys here the King   2215
Seye generally, "Ye are, for every thyng
Alle pardoned." "A, *that* is gode," hire thought,
For heddyngs that the Quene wolde have wrought
Hadde made hir wrecched. Sone they found, bidene,
A Gryphon dormaunt, liggyng in sunne schene,   2220
(An ye wole wite what kinde of creature
A Gryphon is, loketh, lo, the peinture.)

"Uppe, sloggard!" seyde the Quene, "and tak

This yonge mayde, for I moot hasten bak
And se some execucions I desire,   2225
To meet the Mokke Tortus and require
His historye." Alys ne liked nought
The creatures aspect, but hire thought
She myghte saufloker wayte with hit as goon
Aftyr that sauvage Quene: thus dyde she doon.   2230
    The Gryphon sat uppe and rubbed his ene,
Wacched til oute of sighte was gone the Quene,
And laughed. "Lo, here is game!" hit seyde, and spak
Half to hitself and half to Alys bak.
"What game is this?" quod Alys. "*She*," merrilye   2235
The Gryphon seyde, "alle is hir fantasie:
They never execute no bodie. Come!"
    "They bid me 'Come!'" thought Alys, "alle and some!"
As slowly aftyr hit she dyde hir torn.
"'Do this!' 'Do that!' so oft syn I was born   2240
Ne herde I never!" Fer, in litel space
They saw the Mokke Se-tortus sad of face
Aloon upon a rokke. As they cam ner
Alys coude here him wepe and sighen ther
As breke his hert. She pitied him gret won.   2245
"What sorwe hath he?" asked she the Gryphon.
Nigh as bifore the Gryphon answer made,
"Hit is his fantasie, for sorwe nadde
He now or never. Come!" Than to the Tortus
They went. With tery eyen he loked thus   2250
But seyde no word. "This mayde that stondeth here,"
The Gryphon seyde, "thy historye wolde here.
That is to seye, what hath befallen the
In alle thy lyf that wolde connen she."
    "I shal hit telle to hir," with gronyng depe   2255
The Tortus seyde, "al cause hit as to wepe!
Sitteth both doun, and seyth nought til I end."

They sat hem doun, and nought spak to offend
Til Alys thought "If he biginne nought
I wiste not how to fin he may be brought!"   2260

Atte laste the Mokke Se-tortus seyde, "Alas,
"A trewe Se-tortus formerly I was."
A longe silence folwed. Now and then
The Gyphon groined, as a swyn doth when
Hit routeth, and continuelly the Mokke   2265
Se-tortus sobbed, sittynge on the rokke.
Alys was nigh to standynge uppe to say

"I thank thee for thy story. Have gode day!"
But syn hit semed hir ther *most* come more,
Sat stille, and seyde nought, to here his lore.   2270
    "When we were litel," quod he, calme at laste,
Al somdel sobbed he with sorwe fast,
"We went to schole at se. A sterre-fisshe
For-olde the maister was, as we wolde wisshe,
'Mi Ster' we called him." "For whi, if ster   2275
He nas?" quod Alys. "For he taught a mister!"
The Mokke Se-Tortus answered angrily,
"Forsooth thy wit is litel, verily!"
    "Art not aschamed to ask a questioun
So simple?" quod the Gryphon. Othre soun   2280
They nother made, but sat on gase til she
Sunken binethe the erth wolde almoost be.
At last the Gryphon bade the Tortus say
More of his historye. "Tak not al day,"
The Gryphon seyde, and thus continued he.   2285
    "Yis, though thou mayst hit not bileve, in se
We went to schole—" "I never seyde not,"
Quod Alys. "Nay, thou dydest, wel I wot,"
The Mokke Se-tortus seyde. "Kepe wel thy tonge,"
The Gryphon seyde, "thou waggest hit to longe!"   2290
Ere Alys myght replie. "We hadde," went on
The Mokke Tortus, "beste educacion—
We went forsooth ech daye to schole—" "Ye? *I*—"
Quod Alys, "—went to daye-schole eke: so why
Bihoveth thee so proudly speke of hit?"   2295
    "But with addicions?" he wolde wit,
And herkned somdel ferfully. "Feith, yis,"
Quod Alys, "Frenssch and musike, bothe, ywis,
We lerned." "Wasschyng eke?" the Tortus seyde.
"Certaynly not!" she angrily denayde.   2300
"A," seyde the Mokke Se-tortus with relefe,

"Then was thy schole not gode, to my bilefe,
At *oure* they had at botme of the bille
'Frenssh, musike, *wassching,* added'. That was skille!"
      "Ye neded hit but lite," seyde Alys, "at   2305
The botme of the se!" "To lerne that
No coyn I nadde," the Mokke Se-tortus siked,
"Whether hit liked me or me not liked,
I oonly tok the usual cours." "Which was?"
Wolde Alys wit. "The Prive Roum at bas,   2310
For lernyng, as is skille, Stammer, Wet or Quicke,
And Logge Hit," seyde the Tortus, "nolde I swike,
And then four braunches of Quaad Lyvyng Toun,
To lerne which thy braines sholde astoun,
Asmatik, Mucilage, Geomerie,   2315
Aswolkenesse, which meneth litargie."
"Of this Geomerie I never herde,"
Quod Alys. "What is hit?" The Gryphon ferde
As though astonied, with pawes in ayre.
"Not herde of Gomerie? Thou cunnest fayre,   2320
As I suppos, what going wrecched is?"
"To meve in sadnes sorwefully, ywis,"
Quod Alys doutously. "Thou wiste tho
But thou be gowk what meneth merie go."
      Alys abaist nolde question of hit more,   2325
So torned to the Tortus on the shore
And asked him, "What els had yow to lerne?"
      Quod he, "We studied Mysterye ful yerne,"
And tolde the sujets on his finnes eche,
"Bothe auncien and newefangel, harde to teche,   2330
And with Se-ormista: then Crawling, taught
By an olde congre el at whom we laught,
He cam but onys in a wouke; to Swim,
To Crawl, to Feynt with Toil we lerde of him."
      "What lyk was *that*?" quod Alys. "Nay, my bones   2335

They been to stif to show thee for the nones,"
The Mokke Se-Tortus seyde, "ne dyde the Gryphon
Lere hit." "I lakked tyme to lere theron,"
The Gryphon seyde, "but at an auncien crabbe,
The Clater maister, lerned we to blabbe."   2340
    "I never," quod the Tortus, "went to him."
He siked sad, with tery eyen dim,
"Wlaffyng and Gristbitunge, they say, he taught."
    "In sooth he dyde," the Gryphon answer raught,
And siked also. Than bothe creatures   2345
With pawes hid hir faces, as hir natures
Thus priked hem in hir corages. To chaunge
Hir resouns Alys asked, nor made hit straunge,
"How manie houres lerned ye ech daye
Lessuns?" "First daye ten houres," gan he saye,   2350
The Mokke Se-tortus, "on the next daye nine,
And so ech daye twixt matins and compline."
    "How coryouse a plan!" cryde Alys. "That,"
The Gryphon seyde, as on the sand he sat,
"Is why we call hem lessuns, for they lessyn   2355
Fro daye to daye." "Semeth they then most cessin,"
Quod Alys, wondrying at this newe thought,
"If on th'endlefte daye ye lerned nought
Hit moste been a holie daye?" "Forsooth
Hit was," the Tortus seyde, "ne was us looth."   2360
    "How wrought ye on the twelfte?" egrely
Quod Alys. "Pees!" the Gryphon gan him fersly
Entremeten, "enough of lessuns now.
Telle hir of gamen that we pleyde and how."

The Lopstere-Dans

Lokyng at Alys with a sighe, the Mokke   2365
Se-Tortus sittyng doelful on his rokke
His finnes bak drewe over thwert his ye
But coude not speke for sobbynge drerilye.
"As though a bone wer in his throte," the Gryphon
Seyde, and gan to shake him and strike upon   2370
His bak. The Tortus found his voys at last.
With teres doun his chekes rennynge fast,
He comsed to begin:—"Hit may not be
That thou hast lived muche binethe the se,"
Quod he—("I have not," Alys seyde)—"and eke   2375
Perchance thou dydst not ever meet and speke
Unto a lopstere—" ("Anys I tasted—",
Alys bigan to sey; to stynt she hasted,
And answered, "Nay, never,")—"therfore thou
Ne canst what depe delite affordeth yow   2380
A Lopstere Danse, in five figures and
A square." "That can I not, have here my hand,"
Quod Alys, "sey what kind of danse is hit?"

The Gryphon answered, "No one shal sit,
But first along the se-shore form a line—" 2385
"Two lines, that been seven lesse than nine!"
The Mokke Se-Tortus cryde, "of seles, ling,
Se-tortus, mors marine, and othre thing,
And whan ye clere the geli-fisch away—"
"*That* taketh tyme," the Gryphon seyde, "parfay!"— 2390
"Twyys avaunce—" "Echoon with a lopstere,"
The Gryphon cryde, "to serve as parcenere—"
"Bihoveth so," the Tortus seyde: "twyys
Avaunce, bow to thi parcener, ywis—"
"Chaunge lopsteres, retourn in order clene—" 2395
The Gryphon added. "Then, ye wiste, bidene,"
Continewed the Mokke Se-Tortus, "thrawe—"
"The lopsteres," the Gryphon with his clawe
Flung high gan shout—"as fer into the se,"
The Tortus cryde, "as hurlen hem may ye—" 2400
"Swim aftyr hem!" the Gryphon scremed on high
And smoot the ground with lepes Alys nigh.
"Torn up so doun and thanne upright ageyn,"
The Tortus cryde, "for *dans la mer*, we seyn,"
And dansed wildly on the land. As loude 2405
As myghte be the Gryphon as hit coude
Shriked, "Chaunge lopsteres ageyn!" "Then bak
To land—" and sodeynly the Tortus spak
Stilly and lowe, "thus endeth figure the ferst."
The creatures twayn who had at erst 2410
Lept up and doun as though they had been wood
Sat sad and stil and looked wher Alys stood.
    "Hit may wel be a prettie daunce," quod she.
The Mokke Se-Tortus seyde, "Woldest thou hit se?"
"Gramercy," Alys seyde. "Come, let us try," 2415
The Tortus prayed the Gryphon redily,
"The first figure. We can the Lopstere Daunce

Withouten lopsters daunce! Who shal avaunce
To sing?" "Thou,"quod the Gryphon, "I foryet
The woordes." So solempnely they set   2420
Hir fot, hir paws and trotters, on the ground
And daunced in a cercle Alys round,
Wavyng hir fins and claws to kepe the tyme,
And whan they cam to clos they trod sumtime
Upon hir toos. Slowly and sadly sang   2425
The Tortus this, that in hir eres hit rang:

"Wiltow somdel swifter walken," seyde a whityng to a
    snaile,   2426a
"For a porpeis doth persewe me and he presseth on my
    taile.
The lopsteres and lampreis se how lufly they avaunce!
They are wayting on the wet sand—will ye com and joyne
    the daunce?
  Will ye, nil ye, will ye, nil ye, will ye joyne the daunce?
  Will ye, nil ye, will ye, nil ye, nil ye joyne the daunce?

"Thou ne canst not understonde nor gess how grete will be
    oure glee   2426g
Whan they lacche us up with lopsteres and launce us out to
    se!"
But "To fer" the snaile seyde firmly, "hit forthinketh me
    that chaunce,"
Seyde he thonked the whityng throly but he throng out fro
    the daunce,
  Wolde not, coude not, wolde not, coude not, wolde not joyn
    the daunce.
  Wolde not, coude not, wolde not, coude not, coude not joyn
    the daunce.

"No fors is hit how fer we flee," his scaly freend
    replied,   2426m
"The ferer out of Engelond the ner we nigh to Fraunce,
For shore ther is another shapen on that shires side.
So fere not to faille, dere snaile, but com and joyn the
    daunce.
  Will ye, nil ye, will ye, nil ye, will ye joyne the daunce?
  Will ye, nil ye, will ye, nil ye, will ye joyne the daunce?

  "Gramercy," Alys seyde, "ful worthy is
That daunce to wacche ententyfly," of this

Ful glad they had at last of hit made stay;
"The whityng song is much unto my pay!"   2430
 "To rekenen of whityng, they—" the Mokke
Se-Tortus seyde, and meven gan his blokke,
"I trowe thou hast ere now of whityng sene?"
 "Ye, oft, at din—" quod Alys, and bidene
Stilled hir tong. "I noot wher Din may be,"   2435
The Tortus seyde, "but an thou oft dydst se
A whityng, then thou canst hir bleo wel."
 "Asseuredly I may, the sooth to tel,"
Quod Alys carfully, "I wene they kepe
Hir tailes in hir mouth, kevered depe   2440
In crumes." "As to crumes thou art wrong,"
The Tortus seyde, "for in the waves strong
Crumes shal wassche awei, but trewe hit is
Hir tailes stiken in hir mouth, for this
Resoun—" but here the Tortus shut his ye   2445
And gaped. "Sey," quod he, "the resoun whi."
 "Hit is," the Gryphon seyde, "that they wolde go,
Wolde with the lopsters go daunsynge, and so
Were hurled out to se. Long waye to falle
For hem hit was. Fast in hir mouthes alle   2450
Hir tailes steked, they coude hem not remue."
 "Gramercy," Alys seyde, "ye may wel troue
Of whityng knewe I not so muche bifore."
 "An pleseth the, of hem I can seye more,"
The Gryphon seyde. "As, canst thou tel for whi   2455
Men callen hem whityng?" "Certaynly I,"
Quod Alys, "wondered never. Whi?" "*They doon,*"
The Gryphon seyde, "*the botes and the shoon.*"
Solempnely he spak. In wondyr she
"They doon the shoos," repeted, "in the se?"   2460
"And botes," quod the Gryphon. "What dooth *thine*?
I mene, what maketh hem so bright to schine?"

Alys considered hir shoon and eke
The questioun, and answered, "So thee'k,
Oure fotman useth blackyng, as I leve."　　　　　2465
　　"Binethe the se, I nil you not deceve,"
He ceriously seyde, "with whityng doon
Ben they: now canstow wel." "What ben se-shoon
Made oute of?" Alys wondrynge asked. "Soles
And eles, naturally, as ony foles　　　　　2470
Or schrimpes coude yow seye," impaciently
Replied the Gryphon. Alys seyde, "Had I
The whityng been," for thought she on the songe,
"I sholde have seyde unto the porpeis stronge,
'Stonde bak, I pray! We have no nede of *the*!'"　　　　　2475
　　"Hem nedeth that he goo with hem to se,"
The Tortus seyde. "No wise fissch wolde go
To ony stede without a porpeis." "No?"
Supprised quod Alys. "Certaynly nat,"
The Tortus seyde, "ye maye be sure of that!　　　　　2480
For if a fissch sholde com to *me*, and seye
He wolde goon on pilgrymage that daye,
'With what porpeis?' I sholde of him enquere."
　　"Menestow not 'purpos'?" wolde Alys lere.
The Mokke Se-tortus answered with tene,　　　　　2485
A litel irous, "What I seye I mene!"
The Gryphon added, "We wille gladly here
Thyne aventures that thou hast had here."
　　"I coude myn aventures tellen yow,"
Quod Alys somdel ferfully, "til now,　　　　　2490
Bigynnyng oonly at this morwenyng.
Hit boteth not of yisterdai a thyng
Descryve, for then was I another wight."
　　"Arecche us," quod the Tortus. "Sey, how myght
That be." The Gryphon cryde impaciently,　　　　　2495
"No, aventures firste, for dredfully

Arecchyng spendeth tyme." So she bigon
To telle hir aventures everichon
Fro whanne the White Conynge firste she saw
The astrolabe from forth his male draw.   2500
The twayn so clos ayenst hir throng, this syde
And that, and oped mouth and ye so wyde
That she a litel fered was to stond
And speke betwene, but corage sone she fond.
No word at firste they spake, but herkned wel   2505
Until she toold how to the Catirpel
Repetyng *"Ye bene olde, Sir Berti,"* alle
The woordes comyng otherwise dyde falle,
Whan depe the Tortus brethed and replied,
"Ful coryouse is that!" The Gryphon cried,   2510
"Almoost as coryouse as hit myght be."
     "The woordes otherwise repeted she,"
The Tortus seyde thoughtfully. "I wolde
Heren hir now assaye, be she so bolde,
Som poesie to reherse. Bidde hir begin."   2515
Him thought that under yerde of disciplin
Was Alys to the Gryphon whan he spak.
     "Stand uppe, repete, with handes at thi bak,
'Sleuthe cam beslabered with two slymy eighen.'"
     "The beestes give commaundings more than nighen   2520
Lessouns to seye, as thogh in schole I were,"
Thought Alys. Natheles, she stode uppe there
And comsed to repete hit, but hir hedde
So ful was with the Lopster Daunce bestedde
She scarsely knewe what she gan reherse   2525
And alle the woordes cam oute straungely werse.

"Lopsters cam lardid with two lufly clawes,   2526a
And heyre burnist brune by nightes and dawes,
They laiked in lessoun-tyme and lyked not werke,

But coude roten rimes repete in the derke.
Never sory for sawes they seyde on the sands
They daunced ther derfly with drinke in hir hands.
When toold to repent, they tore hir attire
But mutered and mombled and cralled in the mire." 2526h

"That differeth," the Gryphon seyde, "long weye
From what I when a childe was wont to seye."

"In feith," the Mokke Se-Tortus seyde, "ere this,
I seye, *I* herde hit never, but hit is   2530
Uncnawen robyshe, as hit semeth me."
    Alys seyde naught. Wrecchedly doun sat she,
Hir face hid in hir hands, and wondred sore
If *ought* myght hap in naturel wayes more.
    The Tortus seyde, "I praye she wolde expoun."   2535
    "That can she not, for lakketh hit resoun,"
The Gryphon intremeted hastyflye.
"Repete another vers." "How dasedlye,"
Persèvered the Tortus, "dyde they daunce
With drinke on hand and through the mire avaunce?"   2540
    "Dauncyng beginneth thus," quod she, repentyng
(Lyk the lopsters!) that she meved had this thyng.
    "Go on," the Gryphon seyde ageyn, "repete
This vers: *"I passud thoru a garden swete."*
She durst not disobeie, although certayn   2545
Hit sholde com wrong, and seyde with grete disdayn:

> *"I gamnede through a gardyn grene,*   2546a
> *To pley with a pertriche that perned anewe*
> *Hit was fayrer in favor than freke hath sene*
> *Lyk tyrtull on treo hit sange ful trewe,*
> *Therin was a wight winsum of hewe*
> *With a wrenne on hir wriste that werbled bidene*
> *Though flye hit myghte not for fethers to fewe*
> *And tho quod that quene—"*   2546h

    "What worth is hit beguilen us with vers
Thou nilt expoun? No worth, but the revers!"
The Mokke Se-Tortus then con intremete.
"A more confused thyng I never met!"   2550
    "Yis," quod the Gryphon, "thou hadst best, thenche I,
Cess ther," and Alys dyd so gratefully.

"Another figure of the Lopstere Daunce,"
Continued the Gryphon, "shal we praunce?
Or woldestow rather heere the Tortus sing?"   2555
 "For choys, a song, I praye thee, som gaye thyng,
So gentil wolde the Mokke Se-Tortus be,"
Cryde Alys egrely, so that "Pardee,"
The Gryphon seyde, a litel ire was lafte
Within his maw, "of choyses and of crafte   2560
No man may gess. Sing 'Tortus Schowe', olde frend."
 Depe sighes dyde the Mokke Se-Tortus send,
And comsed in a voys that choked was
By sobyng thus to sing with sory gras:—

  "Bewteous schowe so riche and grene   2564a
  That wayteth in a hote disch clene
  Who for suche fyn delices wolde not bowe?
  Schowe of the evening, bewteous schowe!
  Schowe of the evening, bewteous schowe!
   Bew—ewteous schow—owe!
   Bew—ewteous schow—owe!
  Scho—owe of the e—e—vening,
   Bewteous, bewteous schowe!

  "Bewteous schowe, who careth for fisch,   2564j
  Veneisun, or for another disch?
  Who wolde not give alle for two w
  ares worth only of bewteous schowe?
  Wares worth only of bewteous schowe?
  Bew—ewteous schow—owe!
   Bew—ewteous schow—owe!
  Scho—owe of the e—e—vening,
   Bewteous, bewte—OUS SCHOWE!"   2564r

 "Burdoun ageyn!" the Gryphon cryde, but whanne   2565

The Tortus to repeten hit biganne
Fer of was herde a cry, "The querele now
Beginneth!" "Hast! Com foorth! Of this ynow!"
The Gryphon cryde, caught Alys by the hand,
And ran with hir as tyte upon the land.   2570
They wayted not to heere the songes end.
She gasped as she ran, "What querele wend
We unto?" but the Gryphon answered
No moore but "Cometh foorth!" and hastened
The faster. Febly and more faynt behynde   2575
The mournful wordes folwed on the wynde:—

   "Scho—owe of the e—e—vening, 2576a
    Bewteous, bewteous schowe!"

Who Stal the Tartes?

*E*ch on hir trone sat the King and Quene
Of Hertes whan the twayn arrived bidene.
Gadered about hem was a flok, both bridde
And beest, and pakke of cardes eke, the thridde.   2580
Bifore hem stode, in rachetehes harde
The Knaue, with soudeurs at his syde to warde.
With trompe and scrowe of parchemayn in hand
The White Coninge nigh the King dyde stand.
A disch of tartes on a table lay   2585
In midst the curt, so delitable they
That Alys hungred for hem, and hir thought,
"I wissh the querele doon, and cates brought!"
Ther semed litel hope of that, so she,
To pass the tyme, what round hir was gan se.   2590
     In curt of justice Alys nadde stedde
Ere this, but had of hem in bokes redde.
Hit plesed hir to finde she knewe the name
Of wel nigh ech thyng ther. "Here ginneth game!
A sergeant of the lawe that is," quod she,   2595

"The juge, for on his hed a coife hath he."
     The juge unesi was the King, for as
His royall croun upon his coife was—
Se how he wore hit in the peinture at
This bokes frount—he bar an ugsome hat.   2600
     "And that," hir thought, "is wher the jururs sit,
And those twelf creatures" (skil was hit
To call hem "creatures" syn, ye se,
Som beestes were, and som wer briddes fre)
"I hope been jururs." This last word she seyde   2605
Twyys or thryys to hir selfe, wel payde
Bi cause hir thought, and justly, ther wer fewe
Pucelles yong as Alys was that knewe
The word and what hit ment. But "iuree men"
Was just as gode—or "creatures" then!   2610
     The jururs twelf wrat busily echoon
Upon hir schlates. "What is that they doon?"
She whispred to the Griphon. "Naught is ther
Of evidence, or charge to answer,
For hem to writen, for as yet the querele   2615
Hath not begun." "They writen, faire and wele,
Hir names," whispered the Gryphon, "leste
They sholde foryete hem ere the querele ceste."
     "Goukes!" quod Alys loude and angrily,
But moot hir speche chekkin hastyfly: 2620
"Silence in curt!" cryde out the Whit Coninge.
To spye who durste speke, dyde on the Kinge
His spectacle. To Alys hit was pleyn,
As if above hir shuldres she was fayn
To loken, that the jururs "Gowkes" writ   2625
Upon hir schlatestanes, as was fit,
But oon, she saw, ne coude the word not soun,
And soght his nebors help to write hit doun.
     "Confus and ful unredi," thoughte she,

"Ere querele endeth shal hir writyng be!"   2630
   An jurur had a penne that squeked. This
Myght Alys not endure, as Nature is,
So round the curt she went, and stode bihynd,
And whan she saw hir tyme as swift as wind
Snacched hit from him sodeynly. Alas,   2635
The jurur niste wher hit bicomen was,
(He was the litel Lesarde Bille) and serched
Al about, til atte laste he, wrecched,
Thurghout the daye moste with his finger write,
Which left no merk, and gave him smal delite.   2640
   "Redeth, Heraud, the acusacioun!"
The King commaunded. Loude the trumpes soun
Thryys the White Coninge blased out
And rolling ope the parchemayn scrowe gan shout:—

> *"The Quene of Hertes made som tartes*   2644a
> *Upon a somer daye,*
> *The Knave of Hertes stal those tartes*
> *And toke hem fer awaye!"*

   "Considereth youre verdit," seyde the King   2645
Unto the jururs. "Nay, do no such thing
As yet," the Coninge swiftly seyde. "Ere that
Much werk remaineth." "Calle," the King seyde, "what?
The firste witnesse." With that the Coninge blew
Thre blastes on the trumpe and called anew,   2650
"First witnesse!" Thanne the firste witnesse cam,
Hit was the Haberdashere: "Here I am!"
He held an ale coppe in one hand, and in
That other breed with butre thikke or thin.
"I aske pardoun of your Mageste   2655
For thise thynges that I bring with me:
Whan I was sent for soper nas at end."

"Thou owest to have finissht then, my frend,"
The King seyde, "when didst thou begin the fare?"
    The Haberdashere looked at the Hare,   2660
Who with the Dormous on his arm, bihynd
Him into curt was come. "I kepe in mynd,"
He seyde, "of Merche the fourteenth, doutelesse,
I *leve* hit was." "Fifteenth, ne moore ne lesse,"

The Merche Hare seyde. "Sixteenth," the Dormous seyde.
"Writeth this doun!" the King cryde. That obeyde
The jururs: alle thre dates egrely
They on hir schlatestanes feithfully
Gan write, togider add, and render welle
The taille to schillings (thre) and—can ye telle   2670
How manie pens? The King then bade, "Do of
Thine hat." The Haberdashere answered cof,
"Hit nis nat mine." "*Forstolen!*" cryde the King.
He torned to the jururs who the thyng
Writ doun *instanter*. "Hats I kepe to selle,"   2675
Expound the Haberdashere. "None I telle
Of alle ben mine, a Haberdashere I."

    Here doned the Quene hir spectacle, to spy
Hard at the Haberdashere, who pale grewe
And wrickede. "Give thine evidence trewe,"   2680
The King seyde, "be nat afright, or on stede
Wher standestow I schal thee hadet bede."
This semed not to encourage at alle
The witnesse, for he schifted in that halle
From an fot to that other, looking thus   2685
Unesid at the Quene, and so confus
He bot a grete pece from his ale cup
In stede of from the breed he ment to sup.

    [But he had shrunk, to large he sholde have been
To ben afrayd in curt of King or Queen,   2690
For Alys had to grow to two fot high
To sup with him and gylden kei come nigh,
Then shrink to inches nine ere she might win
The garden, and the curt roum intren in.]

    At just this moment Alys gan to fele   2695
Ful coryous a felyng, which a dele
Beguiled hir, until to growe she fynt
She had bigoon ageyn, and nolde stynt.

So hi hir hed now raughte hir thought she wolde
Arise and leve the curt, but then to holde 2700
Hir place hit semed best while yet roum was
For hir. "I wissche thou dyde not queise me as
Thou dost," the Dormous that bisyde hir sat
Gan seye. "Unnethes may I brethe." "For that,"
Quod Alys mildly, "noon help is, syn I 2705
Am growing." "Ye? Thou hast no riht so hi
To growe *here*," the Dormous seyde. "Waltrot!"
Quod Alys moore boldly, "wistow not
Thou growest eke?" "Forsooth, as resoun is
Growe *I*," the Dormous seyde, "in maner wis, 2710
Not sellic swift and large." Thanne
     angerly
He ros and over thwert the curt in hie
He went. The Quene mene time was
     staring yet
Upon the Haberdashere as she
     set,
And as the Dormous over
     thwert the curt
Departed seyde, in voys
     whose wordes hurt,
"Bryng me," quod she to
     ane official,
"The list of singers at
     the festival."
At that the wrecched
     Haberdashere schok
So hard he dyde his
     shoon of nithe his
     sok.

"Afright or not," quod irously the King,
"Give tyte thine evidence, or I shal bring
Swift execucioun upon thine hede."
    "A povre man, Lord King, I am," in drede
Bigoon the Haberdashere trembling sore,   2725
"Soper I had not yet bigoon, not more
Than sey a wowke, and as the breed was thin,
And a therfore I moot with ale begin—"
    "Begin with ale *when*?" "Sir, alweis, a,
Beginneth ale, iwis, the soper—" "Ha!   2730
Wel knowe I A *beginneth* ale! Dost thenche
I am a daf in al my bredth and lenthe?"
    "I am," he seyde ageyn, "a povre man,
And a and alweis algate fynd I can,
Excepte the Merche Hare seyde—" "I seyde not,"   2735
The Merche Hare entremeted hastyf hot.
    "Thou dydst," the Haberdashere seyde. "Nawhit!
For I denaie hit!" "He denaieth hit,"
The King seyde, "leve and writeth not that part."
    "Algate the Dormous seyde—" thus dyde he start,   2740
The Haberdashere, loking trubled bak
In hap the Dormous eke wolde what he spak
Denaie. The Dormous slepte, and wolde denaie
No thyng. "Theraftyr cut I me, I saye,
More botred breed—" the Haberdashere thus   2745
Wolde witnesse bere, but "What dyde the Dormous,"
An of the jururs asked, "sey?" "Nay, that,"
The Haberdashere seyde, "me minneth nat."
    "Thou *moste*," quod the King, "or executed
Sans mercie shaltow swiftly be!" Low louted   2750
Upon a kne, and let his botred breed
And alecoppe fall as hit were made of leed,
The wrecched Haberdashere, and bigan,
"My lord sir King, I am a povre man."

"Ful povre *spekere* artow," quod the King.   2755
Tho gan an irchoun chere, upon which thing
The curt officials streit supresed him.
(Syn hard that word is and of menyng dim,
I schal expoun how hit was doon. A bagge
Of netes skin with rap at mouthe to gagge   2760
They had, wherin they shoved hevedling
The irchoun. Then they sat on hit.) "Seing
That doon now gladdeth me," thought Alys. "Oft
Of querels have I redde that som on lofte
With loude aplaus the verdit wolde greet,   2765
Which noys in curt dyde swift supresioun meet,
But what hit ment I never coude til now."
    The King seyde, "If no more than this ye know
Of hit, ye may stand doun." "No lower may
I go," the Haberdashere seyde, "this way: 2770
For as of now I am upon the flore."
    "Than *sit* thee doun," the King seyde. "Sey no more."
Than made aplaus that other irchoun fere
And was supresed. "Lo, that endeth here
The irchouns," Alys thought. "This proces now   2775
Schal bettre go than wel." "I make a vow,"
The Haberdashere seyde, "my soper I
Wolde rather enden." With a trubled ye
He loked at the Quene, who redyng was
The list of singers. "Go, I grant the gras,"   2780
The King seyde, and the Haberdashere left
The curt in egre hast, ne wayting eft
To don his shoon. "—and cof take of his heed
Withoute," quod the Quene, but with gode speed
The Haberdashere hied out of sight   2785
Bifore the soudeur him arechen might.

"Calleth the nexte witnesse!" seyde the King.
The nexte witnesse into curt dyd bring
The piper box, and Alys gessed bifore
The witnesse cam, syn people nigh the dore   2790
Nered at oon, that hit the Duchesse coke
Moot be for she the piper aiwhere schoke.
The King commaunded, "Give thine evidence."
    "I nil," quod thanne the coke. In consequence
Beguiled was at dulcarnoun the King   2795
And loked trubled at the White Coninge,
Who seyde, in voys lowe, "The hoveth, Sir,
This witnesse clos examine." "Moste I hir
Examine, then I shal," with sory chere
He sayde. His arms he croysed, frouncing dere   2800
Upon the coke until nigh out of sight
His yen were, and grisly seyde, "Sey right,

Of what ben tartes made?" Quod the coke,
"Of piper, for the more part." Awoke
A slepi voys bihynd and quod, "Triacle."   2805
    "Giveth that Dormous a cardynacle!
Caccheth him by the hals!" scricched the Quene.
"Bihefd that Dormous! Let him not be sene!
Undo that Dormous! Torn that Dormous oute
Of curt! Supres him! Pinche him! Make him loute
And shere his nosethirl heres!" Alle confus
For som minutes was the hoole curt thus
Until the Dormous was cast oute, and whan
Alle had set doun ageyn the coke was gan.
    "No fors!" the King releved seyde. "Calle
The nexte witnesse." In a voys smalle
He addide to the Quene, "*Ye* moot, my dere,
Examine this next witnesse, for I fere
Mine hed hit maketh aken!" Alys than
Wacched the White Coninge how he gan   2820
Famlen about the list, ful coryous
To se what creature, what cat or mous,
The nexte witnes sholde be. "As *yet*," quod she,
"Smal evidence have they." Bithencheth ye
Hir wundrunge when the White Coninge gan rede   2825
In litel voys schrille, but loude at nede,
The name "Alys!"

CHAPITRE XII

Alyses Evidence

Egrely Alys sprang
Up schoutyng "Here!": she had foryete how lang
She lately was bicome, and with the liste
Hir dress the jururs box ere wel she wiste   2830
Gan overset, that alle the jururs felle
Upon the peoples heddes, sad to telle,
That stode below, and there they grovellinge lay
To minne hir on a bacin fisch one day
At aventure she overset. "A, wo!"   2835
She cryde, dismaid, "*excuseth* me!" and tho
She gan to liften hem as tyte she myght
Lest lyk the fisch withouten water dight
And gathered not uppe they sterven sholde
Without hir box, as seemed hir they wolde.   2840
  "The querele," seyde the King in voys ful sterne
"Til alle the jururs in hir propre herne
Ben bak ageyn may not continewe—*alle*,"
With fors repeted he, "as right shal falle,"
And loked hard at Alys as he spak.   2845

She saw that when she put the jururs bak
She set the Lesarde up-so-doun his hed,
Such was hir hast, lest som of hem be ded.
Hit myght not stir, but sadly wave his taile
In malencholie wise, to smal availe.   2850
She toke hit oute and sone set hit right,
"And yet how that this creature is dight,"
Hir thought, "hit signifyeth lite: as wele
Hed uppe or taile wol serve in this querele."

Sone as the jururs somdel kevered were   2855
From ofersetting, schlatestanes there
And pennes in hir handes, ardauntly
They went to werk to write the history
Of how the aventure bifel, alle save
The Lesarde, who hit semed gan to rave   2860
With open mouth, and kiked at the rof.
    "What wiste ye," quod the King to Alys, "of
Alle this matere?" "No thyng," quod she. "No thyng
What swa?" persevered ful hard the King.
    "No thyng what swa," quod Alys. "That," quod he,   2865
"Importeth muche," and torned to the iuree.
To writen this upon hir schlates they
Bigan, but then the White Coninge dyde sey
"Importeth *litel,*" worthschiply, but made
A mowe at him and frouned as he bade.   2870
    "*Litel* importeth, I forsooth wolde mene,"
Hastyfly seyde the King, and then was sene
To mutter lowe, "Muche, litel, litel, muche,"
As thogh to here how best shal sounen suche.
    Som jururs wrat "importeth muche" and som   2875
"Litel importeth." Alys saw, but "Com,"
Hir thought, "of this no fors!" for she bent ner
And oferloken myght hir schlates ther.
    Now "Silence!" cryde the King, who in his boke
Bisily gan inditen. Soon he toke   2880
Hit uppe and from hit redde, "Rewle Two
And fourti. *Everich wight whose highte is mo
Than wel a mile moot fro the curt depart.*"
    They alle at Alys loked. "For my part,"
Quod Alys, "*I* nam not a mile high."   2885
    "Thou art," the King gan seye. "Two miles nigh,"
Added the Quene. "In feith, I shal not go,"
Quod Alys. "Ofer-more, I telle the so,

That rewle nis reguler: thou wroughtst hit now."
"The eldest in the bok, I make a vow,   2890
Hit is," the King gan seye. "Nay, that hit nis,
For then it sholde ben Numbre One, ywis!"
     Pale as a pelet therfor grew the King,
And schette his bok in hast as som fals thyng.
"Considereth youre verdit," in a lowe   2895
And trembling voys to jururs in hir rowe
He seyde. "Wilt plese thy Mageste," in hast
The White Coninge sprang up and cryde, "here fast
Is yet more evidence, for on this ground
This paper taken up was lately found."   2900
     "What seith hit?" quod the Quene. "Hit nis not ope
As yet, " the Coninge seyde, "nathles, I hope
Hit ben a lettre, that the prisoner
To—to som wight wrat." "Hit most in that maner
Be written," quod the King, "excepte to no   2905
Wight was hit writ, as selde thou wist is so."
     A jurur seyde, "To whom directed is
This lettre?" "Nay, there no direction nis,"
The White Coninge seyde, "upon the *verso*
Naught is writ." Whan he torned to the *recto*   2910
And oped uppe the paper as he spak,
"This nis no lettre," quod he, "front or bak,
Som proces writ in vers hit is." "Is hit
The prisoneres script that ther is writ?"
An other jurur asked. "Hit is not,"   2915
The White Coninge seyde, "and that, I wot,
Is straungest thyng of alle." (Beguiled wer
The jururs everichoon.) "The prisoner
Som other mannes script hath copied,
I wene," quod the King. (The juree led   2920
To that conclusion loked bright ageyn.)
     "Bileveth me, Sir King," the Knave gan seyn,

"I wrat hit not, nor can they prove that same,
For at the end ther seined nis no name."

"If thou thy name seined not," the King   2925
Gan sey, "the werse hit is. Som wicked thyng
Certayn entendedstow, for hadst thou been
Honest thou woldest let thy name be seen."

The curt in general hir handes smoot
In commendacion, for this they woot   2930
The firste thyng witti was the King that day
Had seyde. "Forsooth," the Quene then gan say,
"That *proveth* that he gilti is. Of with—"
"Nawhit that proveth oght," seyde Alys stith.
"Of what is in this verses, lasse or mare,   2935
Ye woot namoore than doth a dok or stare."

"Redeth hem," seyde the King. The White Coninge
His spectacle dyde on. "I praye, Sir King,"
Quod he, "at whiche place shal I beginne?"

"Begin," the King ful sternly gan him minne,   2940
"At the beginning, go on to the ende,
Then stop." While that the White Coninge hende
Gan rede this verses, and as forth he ferde,
No soun but silence in the curt was herde:—

> They toold me thou hadst been to hir,   2944a
>   And spak of me to him:
> She preysed me a virtuous VIR
>   But seyde I coude nat swim.

> She sent hem word I nadde not gon   2944e
>   (We know that this is so)
> If she sholde hasten thynges on
>   What shal of thee worth tho?

> I gaf hir oon, they gaf him two,   2944i
>   Thou gafst us thre or more;

From him to thee retorned they tho
Al wer they min before.

If I or she perchaunce sholde be   2944m
A part of this matere,
He trusteth the to set hem fre
Restored as we were.

Suppos I dyde that thou hadst bene   2944q
(Before she had this fit)
An obstacle that cam bitwene
Both him, and us, and hit.

Seye not to him she liked hem best,   2944u
For this moot algate be
A secree held from alle the rest
Betwix thiself and me.

"That is the grettest pece of evidence   2945
We have herde yet, and broketh no defence,"
The King seyde, and his handes rubbed, "so,
Letteth the jururs now—" "If ani, lo,
Of hem may hit arecchen," Alys seyde
(So large she was now grown she nas afrayde   2950
To entremetten him), "six pens I shalle
Him give. I gess hit meneth naught at alle."
    The jururs writ upon hir schlatestones
"She gesseth hit meneth naught for the nones,"
But noon assayed to expoun the thyng.   2955
    "If then hit meneth naught," quod tho the King,
"That spareth us labour, and toil and care,
No menyng nede we seke." He then gan stare
With on ye fast upon the verses spradde
Above his kne, and seyde, "But if I madde,   2960

Methinketh that som sens I may here se.
'But seyde I coude nat swim—' That meneth the,"
He added tornyng to the Knave, "for loke,
Thou canst not swim, canstow?" He sadly schoke
His heved. "Semeth hit, to loke on me,   2965
I can?" (In feith, hit semed *not*, for he
Of paper bord constructed fully was.)

    "So far, so gode," the King seyde, mutring as

He redde: " *'We know that
    this is so'*—parfay,
That is the iuree, sittinge
    here today—
*"'If she sholde hasten
    thynges on'*—I wene
That moot forsooth be no
    one but the Quene—
*'What shal of thee worth
    tho?'*—Ye, what?—*'I
    gaf
Hir oon, they gaf him
    two'*—No doute I haf
That moot be what he with
    the tartes dyde!"

"But therupon we reden," Alys cryde,
'*From him to thee retorned they tho.*'" "Whi, ther
They are!" the King gan glefully auer,
And pointed to the tartes on the table.
"Clerer to show than *that* no thing is able.   2980
And then ageyn, '*Before she had this fit*'—
I trow no yvel fits have ever hit
Thee, dere?" he seyde to the Quene. "Whew,
Never!" the Quene seyde furiously, and threw
At the Lesarde as she spak a botel ink   2985
Ere wrecched litel Bill myght bend or blink.
(No longer with one finger on his schlate
He wroot: no mark hit made, he foond of late;
But now he hastyflye began ageyn
Using the ink that on his face lyk reyn   2990
Was rennyng doun, while that hit lasten myght.)
    "The woordes *fit* not thee, I sey outright,"
The King seyde, smilyng round the curt. Silence.
"A mirie geste to you I dyde dispence,"
The King seyde wrathfully; then laughed they alle.   2995
"Ageyn upon the jururs now I calle,
Hir verdit to consideren," gan saye
The King, for nigh the twentieth tyme that daye.
    "Nay!" quod the Quene. "Sentence first—verdit after."
    "Waltrot!" seyde Alys loude. "Hit maketh lahter   3000
To thench of sentence first." "Holdeth youre tunge!"
The Quene with purpre face seyde and wrunge
Hir hondes. "I shal not," quod Alys cof.
    "Of with hir hed!" schriched the Quene. "Have of!"
But no wight meved. (She to ful stature now   3005
Was grown): "Who careth," Alys quod, "for *yow*?
Naught but a pakke of cardes ben ye alle!"
    Into the ayre the hoole pakke rose, to falle
On hir. A litel crie she made, of fryght

And ire, and tried to bete hem of dounright   3010
And foond hir liggyng on the bank, hir hed
Upon hir sosters lap. Som lefes ded
That from the trees on Alys face, parfay,
Had flotred doun she gently bruscht away.
    "Awak, dere Alys!" seyde hir soster. "Why,   3015
How long a slepe thou hast had, certaynly!"

"So coryouse a sweven have I met,"
Quod Alys, and so wel as she myght yet
Hir minne of hem she told hir soster alle
The Aventures straunge that dyde befalle   3020
As ye have rede before, and at the end
Hir soster gan hir kisse, and homward send.
"A coryouse sweven *was* hit, dere," quod she,
"But run in now for souper; thou mayst se
How late hit is." So Alys ros and ran,   3025
And while she ran hir thought, as wel she can,
How ful of wondyr had hir sweven bene.

E P I L O G U E

But stille hir soster sat, and yet gan lene
As Alys went hir hed upon hir hand,
To wacche the settyng sun and derked land,   3030
And thenche on litel Alys and hir dreme,
How wonderful hir Aventures seme,
Til she to met in ferly wise and this
Hir sweven was, I sey hit as hit is:—
    Of litel Alys atte first met she,   3035
Smal hands ageyn were clasped on hir kne
Bright egre yes loked up at hir—
She herde hir verie voys, and saw the stir
She gaf hir hed to kepe the wandryng here
From out hir yes that *wolde* algate com there—   3040
And as she herkned, or so met, the wyde
Hoole place around hir quikened at that tyde
With alle the straunge creatures that dyde seme
To pleyen in hir litel sosters dreme.
    The long gras russled at hir fet: the White   3045
Coninge hit was that hied by as tyte—
The ferful Mus that splasshed thurgh the pol

Harde by—the ale coppes ratelen fol
Or emti herde she as the Merche Hare
And frends hir never ending soper pare,   3050
The Quenes schrille voys that biddeth gon
Hir gestes sad to execucion—
Ageyn on Duchesse kne the pig babi
Gan nese, while platters crased round his ye—
Ageyn the Gryphon scricched, and with quille   3055
The Lesarde latte his sclatestane eres thrille,
Supresed irchouns choked, while fro fer
The Mokke Tortuses sobbynge menged ner.
    So stille she sat, with yes shut, and myght
Have thought hir self in Wondyr Lond that nyght,   3060
Al knew she that she needed but hem ope
And alle sholde chaunge ageyn, as one moot hope,
To dulle familarité—the gras
Sholde oonly rutelen in the wind, alas,
The pol sholde ripelen but as waved the reedes—   3065
The ratelyng coppes chaunge to wher on medes
Shepe belles tinclen, and the Queens schrille crie
To schephirde boyes voys—nesyng of babi,
Scricche of the Gryphon, and ech other soun
Sholde chaunge, she knewe, within the bisy toun   3070
To alle his menged noys—kynes fer lowynge
Sholde be the Mokke Tortuses gret sobbynge.
    And last, in hir imaginacyon
She saw in aftyr tymes many on
This same litel soster woman growen   3075
Sholde kepe thurgh alle the riper yeres bestowen
Hir simple lovyng hert as when a child;
And gader round hir other children mild,
And make *hir* yes bright and egre as
She toold hem straunge tales, eke per cas   3080
The dreme of Wondyr Lond of longe ygoon;

Felyng hir simple sorwes everichoon,
Glad in hir simple joys, that sholde hir minne
Hir childhode dayes, the happi someres inne.

Glossary

(Unreferenced words may be sought in the introductory poems)

a *adv.* always, 2728
a! *interj.* ah!, 668, 753
abaist *pp.* abashed, 2325
Abigail *n.* typical name for a serving maid *(called after King David's most domesticated wife and subservient "handmaid", 1 Samuel 25:40-41)*, 210
abregge *v.* cut short, abridge, 856
abreyde *v. pt.* awoke, 216, 325, 969
abrood *adv.* abroad, all round, 948
abuf *prep.* above, 1486
abyde *v.* wait, 710
accordaunt *adj.* agreeable to, in accordance with, 2037
acqueynte *v.* make acquainted, introduce, 2008
acquit *pp.* acquitted, absolved, 1353
acusacioun *n.* accusation, 2641
addicions *n. pl.* additions, extras, 2296
admitin *v.* admit, 487
adoun *adv.* down, 492
adrest *pp.* approached, 916
aferde *pp.* afraid, 219, 784
afered *v. pt.* frightened, 460; *pp.* 687, 913
affray *n.* fright, 420
afright *pp.* frightened, 1653
aftyr Englyssh later English
agast *pp.* horrified, 134, 1375
agayn *prep.* against, 1069

agreen *v.* agree, 483
aha! *interj.* aha!, 1079
ahem! *interj.* ahem! *(pun on "a (h')M")*, 1740
aither ... or *conj.* either...or, 43
aiwher *adv.* everywhere, all over, 215, 1091, 2792
ajourne *v.* adjourn, 521
ajuged *v. pt.* judged, declared, 1028, 1984
aken *v.* ache, 2819
al¹ *adv.* although, 407, 2272
al², **alle** *n.* all, 47, 332 **al and som(e)** *n. phr.* all there is to it, the whole matter, 792
alas! *interj.* alas, 340, 360 **alas and weilaway** *interj.* Oh dear! *(strong lamentation)*, 374
alembike *n.* alembic, retort *(vessel for receiving distilled vapour)*, 960
algate *adv.* always, at any rate, 61, 605, 734
alle see **al²**
aller *adj.* of all **aller beste** best of all, 658
almicanteras *n.* notional circle describing altitude, 85
aloon *adv.* alone, 361, 661
alweis *adv.* always, 2729 **alwey** *adv.* 633
amiddes *adv.* among, 896
amyable *adj.* friendly, 1393

an[1] *num.* one, 296, 720, 833

an[2] *conj.* if, 425

anewe *adv.* afresh, 564

angels *n. pl.* angles, corners, 1824

anon *adv.* at once, 265, 1576

anorned *pp.* adorned, 1825

anoye, anoy *n.* annoyance, 424, 510, 1316c

antiphoners *n. pl.* responding choristers, 93

anys *adv.* once, 2377

apayde, apayd *pp.* pleased, 371, 1109

apelin *v.* appeal, 2053

apert *adv.* apart, 1076

aplaus *n.* applause, 2765

apparaunce *n.* re-appearance, 1440

appelen *v.* accuse, 606c

appere *v.* appear, 162, 920

approchen *v.* approach, draw near to, 1176

apt *adj.* ready, able, 490

archebischop *n.* archbishop, 508f

ardauntly *adv.* eagerly, diligently, 2857

arecche *v.* explain, 974, 2494

arecchyng *verbal n.* explaining, 2497

arechen *v.* reach, arrest, 2786

ares *n. pl.* oars

areste *v.* arrest, capture, 636

argumentatyf *adj.* argumentative, 482

arre *adj.* former, 1667

arsmetrike *n.* arithmetic, 335, 1312

artow (art + thou) *v. phr.* are you?, 804, 994

arum *n.(Northern)* arm, 812

as as as breke his hert *adv. phr.* as though his heart were breaking, 2245 as he were *adv. phr.* as if he were, 556 as liked hem *adv.phr.* as they pleased, 545 as man had *adv. phr.* as a man who had, 318 as tyte *adv. phr.* swiftly, 317, 1327

aschamed *pp.* ashamed, 2279

Asia *n.* Asia (*Asia Minor, modern Turkey*), 508e

asmatik *n.* asthmatic, 2315

aspect *n.* appearance, looks, 2228

assaye[1] *n.* essay, attempt, 789

assaye[2], assay *v.* try, test, 82, 334, 403 assaid *v. pt.,* 1282

asseuredly *adv.* assuredly, certainly, 2438

astonied *pp.* astonished, 692

astoun *v.* astonish, 2314

astrolabe *n.* astrolabe (*instrument for measuring the angles of the stars*), 22, 2500

aswolkenesse *n.* sloth, indolence, 2316

at do *adv. phr.* ado, going on, 563

atte last *adv. phr.* at (the) last, 484, 589

attemprelye *adv.* attemptingly, 1890

attempten, *v.* try, attempt, 1816

atteyne *v.* attain, get to, 902

attle *v.* intend, 1008

auctor *n.* author, 1391

aught *v. pt.* owned, 2066 the aught *v. impers.* you ought, 234

auncien *adj.* ancient, 2330

aunters *n. pl.* adventures, 768

auer *v.* aver, maintain, 2978

availe *n.* avail, help, 2850

avaunce *v.* advance, come forward, 492, 1614

aventure *n.* adventure, 2859; *n. pl.* 2488, 3020 at aventure by chance, 1803, 2835; *v.* risk, 1174

avis *n.* advice, 235 avys *n.* 508g

avysed *pp.* advised, informed, 1369

awayted *pp.* waited for, 544

axe[1] *n.* axe, 1026ee, 1306

axe[2] *v.* ask, 1305

ayenst *prep.* against, 1074

ayre *n.* air, 100, 798

babee *n.* baby, 1261 Babees bok *n.* children's advice book (*babies' book*), 420

Babel *n.* Babel (*site of the confusion of tongues*), 832

Babelynge *n.* Babylon (*the wicked city*), 344

babi *n.* baby, 3053

bacin *n.* basin, bowl, 2834

bakkes *n. pl.* bats, 115

bar *v. pt.* bore, endured, 2115

bas *n.* base, bottom, 2310

baser *n.* executioner, 2025

bede *v.* bid, command, 2682; *v. pt.* bade, commanded, 2192

been, ben *v.* be, 504; *pp.* been, 1379

beestes *n. pl.* beasts, 190, 267; *posses.* 476

befalle, befall *v.* happen, 254, 396

beguiled *v. pt.* bewildered, puzzled 1003 beguileth *v.3 sing.*, 334

bek *v.* nod, beckon, 1026aa

ben *see* been; *see* bene

bendicite! interj. (Latin) indeed (*a blessing*), 643

bene, ben *v.* are 321, 1903

bent[1] *n.* ground, place on bent there, 44

bent[2] *pp.* resolved, determined (to go), 1143

bere *v.* bear, 375, 839

berke *v.* bark, 907; *n.* barking, 931

berne *n.* barn, 456

besiship *n.* business, 1797

beslabered *pp.* bespattered, dirty, 2519

best *n.* beast, 1874

bestedde *pp.* bestead, occupied, troubled, 2524

bestowen *pp.* bestowed, granted, 3076

besy *adj.* busy, 642

bet *adv.* better go bet go quickly, 706, 817

bete *v.* beat, 1097, 3010

beth *v. imper. pl.* be, 1887

betime *adv.* in time, 40

betwix *prep.* between, 434

bidde *v. imper.* bid, command, 2515

bidden *pp.* suggested, directed, 529

bide *v.* dwell, spend time in, 633

bidene *adv.* at once, quickly, 1840; together, 2578; indeed (*rhyming tag*), 2396, 2546f

bifel *v. pt.* happened, 1

bigoon *v. pt.* began, 263

bihefded *pp.* beheaded, 670

bihotest *v. pt.* (you) promised, 593

bihoveth *v. 3 sing.* behoves, suits, 764, 2295 behoveth me *v. phr.* I ought to, 281

bilef *v. pt.* remained, 1895

bileve *v.* believe, 216, 2286 bileved *pp.* 1130 bileveth *v. imper.* (*polite pl.*), 2922

bille *n.* bill (*beak; missive*), 1580

binethe *prep.* under, 554 (*also* nithe)

bischop *n.* bishop, 514

biside *prep.* beside, next to, 560

bisily *adv.* busily, diligently, 1783

bitake *v.* take, convey, 696

bithencheth *v. imper. pl.* imagine, 2824

bitokened *v. pt.* indicated, 399

bityde *v.* happen, 58

blabbe *v.* chatter, 28, 2340

blakeberied *pp.* a blakeberied *adv.phr.* gathering blackberries, wandering, 508d

blancmange, *n.* white meat, 204, 1026n

blased *v. pt.* blew, 2643

bledeth *v. 3 sing.* bleeds, 198

blee, bleo *n.* face, appearance, 1185, 2437

blerily *adv.* blear-eyed, 1658

bleteth *v. 3 sing.* bleats, 348h

blew[1] *v. pt.* blew, 1051

blew[2] *adj.* blue, 949

blinne *v.* cease, 1263

blokke *n.* bulk, body, 2432

blubred *v. pt.* bubbled, 959 blubren *v.* bubble, 1053

bobbaunce *n.* arrogance, 516f

bobet *n.* blow, 1926

bok *n.* book, 4

bon chance *adv. phr.* good luck, 749

bonkes *n. pl.* banks, 1107

boot *n.* advantage, 402, 1902

bord *n.* board, 104

bore *n.* boar, 1026q

borwe *n.* pledge hat to borwe *n. phr.* I'll bet my hat (*a strong assertion*), 693

bot *v. pt.* bit, 2687

boterflie *n.* butterfly, 989

botes *n. pl.* boots, 2458

boteth *v. 3 sing.* helps, 1253

botred *pp.* buttered, 2745

boun *adj.* bound to, ready to, 690

brag *v.* boast, 170

bras *n.* brass, 698

brayn wode *adj. phr.* violently mad, 1453

breken, breke *v.* break, 732 breke *v.pt.* broke, 1235; *v. subjunctive* would break, 2245 al to breken *v. phr.* smash to pieces, 1216

bren *v.* burn 195, 869 brennyng *pres. part.* burning, 29

brent *pp.* burnt, 190

brethles *adj.* breathless, 930, 2207

briddes *n. pl.* birds, 267; *posses. pl.* birds', 160

briht *adj.* bright, colourful, 1780

broche *v.* break into, broach, 1474

broketh *v.3 sing.* deserves, 2946

brook *v.* enjoy **brook … hat** *v. phr.* a strong assertion, equivalent to "upon my life" etc., 180

broun *adj.* brown, 32, 126 **brune** *adj.* 450, 2526b

bruscht *v. pt.* brushed, 3014

bucket *n.* bucket, 756

bule *n.* bull, 348f

bulk *n.* trunk, body, 1026z

burdoun *n.* burden, chorus, 1318, 2565

burnist *adj.* burnished, polished, 2526b

but *conj.* but, 569; unless, 364, 498, 602; *adv.* only, 396, 623

butre *n.* butter, 1548, 2654

cacchen, cacche *v.* catch, 113, 436 **cacche** *v. imper.* 855 **caccheth** *v. imper. pl.* 2807

cake *n.* cake, 269

cam *v. pt.* came, 268

camomille *n.* camomile, 2096

can *v.* can, 325; know, 114, 408, 525

cardynacle *n.* heart attack, palpitation, 1676

cared *v. pt.* took care, 35

cas *n.* case, condition, 474

cast *v.* threw, 317 **cast in mynd** *v. phr.* considered, 327

casus vocativus *n. phr.* (*Latin*) vocative case (*form of noun used to address someone or something*), 411

cates *n. pl.* delicacies, titbits, 2588

catirpel *n.* caterpillar, 949, 953

caught *pp.* caught, inferred from, 889

Caunterbury *n.* Canterbury, 508g

cautelously *adv.* cautiously, 1598

cercle *n.* circle, 541, 591, 2422

ceriously *adv.* seriously, meticulously, 1368, 2467

certayn *adj.* certain, 2545; *adv.* certainly, 494; **certaynly** *adv.* 1660

cese *v.* cease to, desist from, 1104; *v. imper.* 1751

cessin, cess *v.* cease, 2356, 2552 **ceste** *v. pt.* ceased, 2618

chaffare *n.* business, bargaining, 384, 1190

chambre *n.* room, 715

chasen *v.* chase, 871, 899

chasteyn *adj.* chestnut, 1388

Chaucer *n.* Geoffrey Chaucer, 14th-century poet, 555

chaunce *n.* chance, opportunity, 2426i

chaunge *n.* change, 970 **chaunged** *v. pt.* changed, 323

chayr *n.* chair, 1493

chef *adj.* chief, main, 478

chekes *n. pl.* cheeks, 319

chekkin, chek *v.* check, stop, 182, 2620

chepe *n.* bargain, cheap, 1026p, 2169

chere *n.* aspect, facial expression, 582, 628; *v.* cheer, 2756

chese *v.* choose, 1650

Chestre *n.* Chester, town in Cheshire in N.W. England, 1271

cheven, cheve *v.* achieve, gain, 252, 1076

cheyne *n.* chain, 11

childgered *pp.* childlike, 1026m

childli *adj.* childlike

chimnee *n.* chimney, 745

chiries *n. pl.* cherries, 203

chivered *v. pt.* shivered, 503

choys *n.* choice, 1240, 2186 **by choys** *adv. phr.* deliberately, 460

choysest *adj.* favourite, 1545

chylindre *n.* cylindrical pocket sundial, 1541

clap *n.* clap, stroke, sudden noise **at a clap** suddenly, 260

clater *v.* clatter, jabber, 2340

clause *n.* phrase, 534

clawen *v.* scratch, 436 **clawes, claws** *n.* claws, 1394, 2423

clere *adj.* clear, obvious, 19; *v.* clear, sweep, 2389

clerk *n.* clerk, learned person, clergyman, 491

cloistre *n.* cloister, 633; *v.* 387

clom! *interj.* hush!, 346

clong *v. pt.* clung, 476

clos *adj.* close, near, 476; *adv.* 796, 2424

clubbes *n. pl.* clubs, 1822

cnawe *v.* know, 988
cof *adv.* quickly, 782, 1956
cognisaunce *n.* realization, 1118
coife *n.* coif (*cap surrounding head, worn by serjeants at law*), 2596
cointly *adv.* cunningly, prudently, 1899
cok *n.* cock, 241
coke *n.* cook, 1256
coked *pp.* cooked, 2211
colerik, colrik *adj.* irascible, 484, 2094
commaunde *n.* command, 670
commaunded *v. pt.* ordered, 2793
commaundings *n.* orders, 2520
commendacion *n.* approval, 2930
commende *v.* commend, act graciously, 1724
companye *n.* company, 473
complexioun *n.* complexion, mixture (*of bodily "humours"*); make-up, consistency, 1680
compline *n.* evening church service, 2352
comprehende *v.* understand, 1639
comsed *v. pt.* began, managed, 646, 2373
con¹ *v.* can, 1474, 1489
con² *v.* know, 2004
conceptioun *n.* idea, 1127
conceyve *v.* conceive, imagine, 1680
concilie-rese *n.* council election, caucus race, 530
confit *n.* sweetmeat, 53
confortlesse *adj.* uncomfortable, 1486
confus *adj.* confused, 864, 981
confyts *n. pl.* sweetmeats, 566
congre el *n.* conger eel (*large species of eel*), 2332
coni clapper *n.* rabbit warren, 354
coninge *n.* rabbit, 13, 308
coningere *n.* rabbit hole, warren, 32
conned *v. pt.* studied, learnt
connen *v.* know, 2254
conninge *n.* knowledge, learning, 81
connyng *n.* learning, 486, 1302; *adj.* clever, 889
constreyned *pp.* forced, constrained, 1227
continuely *adv.* continually, 384
contrarious *adj.* contrary, in the opposite way, 1430

contritely *adv.* contritely, repentant, 299
cop *n.* top, 947
coppe *n.* cup, 1715 coppes *n. pl.* cups, 3048
corage *n.* courage, 1871 corages *n. pl.* hearts, dispositions, 2347
cordial *n.* stimulating drink, 726
cors *n.* body, 1732
cortayse *n.* courtesy, politeness, 1703
cortayslye *adv.* courteously, 505
cortin *n.* curtain, 152
coryouse *adj.* curious, 207, 321, 725
coryouser *adv.* more curiously, 271
cotage *n.* cottage, 351
couard *n.* coward, 821
coude *v. pt.* could, 8; knew how to, 101; knew, 335, 1006
coudest *v. 2 sing.* (you) could, 1615
countenaunce *n.* countenance, expression, 1634
countrepleted *pp.* contradicted, 1039
coured *v. pt.* cowered, 1152
cours *n.* course, 541, course of study, 2309 bi course *adv. phr.* of course, 1733
courtois *adj.* courteous, 1914
coyn *n.* coin, money, 2307
crabbe *n.* crab, 627
crafte, craft *n.* craft, art, accomplishment, 997, 2560
craftmon *n.* craftsman, 348d
cralled *v. pt.* crawled, 2526h
crased *v. pt.* cracked, broke, 3054
crasshe! *interj.* crash!, 841
craven *adj.* cowardly, 821
cremesin *adj.* crimson, 1837
crepe *v.* creep, 253, 1951
crewe *n.* crew, crowd of creatures, 563
Cristes messe *n.* Christmas
croppes *n. pl.* crops, treetops, 1095
croslet *n.* crucible, 1052 croslets *n. pl.* 961
croud¹ *n.* crowd, 468
croud², croude *v.* thrust, 1302, 1489
croune, croun *n.* crown, 516d, top of head, 1624b
croys *n.* cross, 347 croysed *v. pt.* crossed, 2800
crucken *v.* crook, 2082

crulled, crulle *adj.* curled, 330, 1187; *v.* *pt.* 743

crulles *n. pl.* curls, 1200

crumes *n. pl.* crumbs, 2441

crye *v.* cry, call out, 559

cucumers *n. pl.* cucumbers, 801

cukkow *n.* cuckoo, 346, 348b; fool, 348k, 1730

cunnen *v.* know, 1275

cuntre *n.* country, 342

cure *n.* care, 532, 1294

curiuser *adv.* more curiously, 271

curt *n.* court, 2586

curteislye *adv.* courteously, 99

curteoures *n. pl.* courtiers, 718, 1825

Cytherea *n.* the planet Venus, 1303

daf *n.* idiot, 1253, 2732

daffy *adj.* idiotic, 616

dagged *pp.* bedraggled, ragged, 475

daintees *n. pl.* dainties, sweetmeats, 2098

dais *n.* dais (*platform where stood the high table where nobles dined*), 1026r

danse, dans *n.* dance, 2381 *also* daunce

dans la mer *prep. phr.* (*French*) in the sea, 2404

dansed *v. pt.* danced, 2405

Dante *n.* Dante, 14th-century Italian poet, whose *Divina Commedia* depicts Satan firmly stuck at the centre of the earth, 77

dassche, dasche *v.* dash, fall suddenly, 378, 842

dasedlye *adv.* giddily, in a daze, 2538

datheit! *interj.*(*Northern*) a curse on!, 812

daunce *n.* dance, 386

daungerous *adj.* reluctant, 1178

dawenyng *n.* dawn, 1638

dawes *n. pl.* days, 1667

dayesyes *n. pl.* daisies, 10

debat *v.* debate; converse, argue, 966

deceyued *pp.* deceived, cheated, 240

dede *n.* deed, 581

defaute *n.* default, 313

degre *n.* degree, extent, 8

degree *n.* order, 1958

dele, del *n.* deal, amount, 1146, 2696

deliberedly *adv.* deliberately, after thought taken, 957

delices *n. pl.* delights, delicacies, 2130, 2564c

delitable *adj.* delectable, 2586

delite *n.* delight, 1079

deliver *adj.* athletic, 1026o

delivered *pp.* rescued, 504

delved *v. pt.* dug, 2123

demde *v. pt.* condemned, 2202

deme *v.* deem, judge, 102, 6061 demed *v.* *pt.* 367

demestow *v.2 sing.* (demest + thou) thou judgest, you think, 1594

denaie *v.* deny, 2738 denaieth *v.3 sing.* denies, 2738 denayde *v. pt.* denied, 2300

dent *n.* blow, thunderclap, 1622b

denye *v.* refuse, 606d

depaynt *pp.* depicted, 555

depe *adj.* deep, 304, 2255

dere¹ *adj.* dear, 429 deres *n. pl.* dears, 277

dere² *adv.* fiercely, 2800

derfly *adv.* boldly, 2526f

derk *adj.* dark, 47

derke *n.* dark, darkness, 318

descenden *v.* descend, 381

descryve *v.* describe, 2493

despeire *n.* despair, 565

devyse *v.* devise, 904

dewe *n.* dew, 1072

deyntee *adj.* dainty, 434

diamants *n. pl.* diamonds, 1826

diffred *v. pt.* differed, 2157

digestioun *n.* digestion, 2127

diggand *pres. part.* (*Northern*) digging, 807

dighte *adj.* prepared, arranged, made up, 78, 1479

dim *adj.* dark, obscure, faint, 931, 2758

dine *v.* dine, have dinner, 1150

dinge *v.* strike, 865

dint *n.* blow, 865, thunder clap, 2184

direccioun *n.* direction, 1413

dische *n.* dish, 1238

disciplin *n.* discipline, 2516

discomfort *n.* discomfort, 477

disdayn *n.* disdain, dislike, 2546

disesperat *adj.* desperate, despairing
(hopeless), 310

dismaid *pp.* dismayed, 2836

dismally *adv.* gloomily, 1556

dispence *v.* give out, distribute, 2994

dispitously *adv.* angrily, scornfully, 623

displayde *v. pt.* presented, displayed, 506

displesaunce *n.* displeasure (*punning on
Alice Liddell's middle name, Pleasance*),
1754

disport *n.* sport, pleasure, 382

disputacioun, disputicioun *n.* dispute,
disagreement, argument, 1964, 2017

distantz *n.* distance, 84

distourbed *pp.* disturbed, 423

distourbled *pp.* troubled, 645

disturben *v.* disturb, 1087

divined *v. pt.* understood, interpreted
(prophesied), 674

doelful *adj.* doleful, mournful, 2366

doghter *n.* daughter, 628

dois *v. 3 sing.* (*Northern*) does, 815

dok *n.* duck, 469, 2936

dom *adj.* dumb, 2212

don *v.* (do + on) put on, 2783 doned *v.
pt.* donned, put on, 2678

donat *n.* elementary Latin grammar
textbook (*after the Latin author
Donatus*), 405

done *v.* do, 614, 1990

doon *v.* do, 537, 2457

dore *n.* door, 143, 1781

dormaunt *adj.* ready laid, 1480; still,
stationary (*in heraldic posture*), 2220

dostow *v.* (dost + thou) are you doing?,
684, 805

dounright *adv.* downright, entirely, 3010

doute *v.* doubt, fear, 712

doutelees, douteles *adv.* doubtless, 70,
1645

doutously *adv.* doubtfully, 2323

douvre *n.* rabbit burrow, 1546

drad *v. pt.* dreaded, feared, 94

draf *v. pt.* drove, thrust, 1254

drasty *adj.* rubbishy, 1026cc

dred[1] *n.* fear, 94, 472

dred[2] *adj.* frightful, 1962

drede *v.* fear, 314

dredfully *adv.* dreadfully, 2496

dreme *n.* dream, 3031

drerilye *adv.* drearily, sadly, 2368

drery *adj.* dull, tedious, 516 drery fare *n.
phr.* wretched condition, 361

drewe *v. pt.* drew, inscribed, 541

driest *adj.* driest, 502

drou *v. pt.* drew, drained

drublie *n.* (*Northern*) trouble, 820

drusi *adj.* drowsy, 116

drye[1] *v.* dry, 479 dryeth *v. 3 sing.* dries,
518

drye[2] *adj.* dry, 494, 517

duces *n. pl.* leaders, 502d

duchesse *n.* duchess, 667

dul *adj.* dull, 262

dulcarnon *n.* bewilderment, 565, 1063

durste, durst *v. pt.* dared, 202, 2622

duven *v.* dive, 31

dwelleth *v.3 sing.* lives, abides, 448

ech *adj.* each, 381 eches *n. poss.* each
one's, 568

Ector *n.* Hector of Troy (*like Charlemagne and King Arthur, one of the
"Nine Worthy"*), 1668

ee *n.* eye, 782, 1096

effectyf *adj.* effective, 522

eft *adv.* after, again, 2782

egge *n.* edge, 948

egges *n. pl.* eggs, 1113

egrely *adv.* eagerly, 639

eighen *n. pl.* eyes, 2519 *also* eyen

eke *adv.* also, 9, 444

elbowe *n.* elbow, 742

elde *v.* grow old, 771

eles *n. pl.* eels, 2470

elles, els *adv.* else, 105, 514

empryse *n.* undertaking, 956

emti *adj.* empty, 3049

enclynyng *verbal n.* inclination, falling,
61

endite *v.* compose, 765

endlefte *num. adj.* eleventh, 2358

ene *n. pl.* eyes, 2231 (*also* eyen, yes)

eni *adj.* any, 1983

enjoined *v. pt.* demanded, directed, 2013

enlumined *v. pt.* illuminated, lit up, 140

enow *adj.* enough, 245 (*also* ynow)

enquered *v. pt.* inquired, 509, 1795

entendedstow *v. pt.* (entendedst + thou)
you intended, 2927

ententyfly *adv.* attentively, 2428

enter *adj.* entire, 264

entree *n.* entry, entrance, 1334

entremeten *v.* interrupt, interfere, 1706,
2363

erande *n.* errand, 706 erandes *n. pl.*
errands, 714

ere¹ *n.* ear, 1921 eres *n. pl.* ears, 135

ere² *adv.* before, 152, 652

erle *n.* earl, 502f

errour *n.* mistake, 689

erst *adv.* first, formerly, 26, 2117

ese *v.* ease, comfort, 1314

esi *adj.* easy, 547

eske *v.* ask, 1514

espie *v.* espy, 24

ete *v.* eat, 585, 913 ete *v. pt.* ate, 269

evanisshed *pp.* disappeared, 2075

even *adj.* equal, the same, 1636

everichoon *pr.* every one, 348i

excepte *conj.* unless, 2905

exempli gratia n. phr. (*Latin*) for
example, 194, 1605

expound *v.* explain, 540, 689

eyen *n. pl.* eyes, 449, 1738 (*also* eighen,
ene, yes)

fade *adj.* faded, dim, 2073 fadeth *v.3
sing.* withers, 348c

faire *adv.* handsomely, well, 450;
successfully, 1350

fal *v.* fall, happen, 725

fals *adj.* false, untrue, 1127

familarite *n.* familiarity, 3063

famlen *v.* fumble, 2821

fantasie *n.* imagination, 707, 2236

fare *n.* proceeding, business, 361, 2659

faren *v.* go, 1223 farewel *v. phr.* (*go well*)
goodbye, 275

fast *adj.* stuck, shut, 923; *adv.* firmly,
1731; quickly, 2272; close by, 2898

faste *adv.* close by, 576

favored *pp.* preferred, favourite, 2179

favour *n.* approval, 502b

fay *n.* faith, 1522 in fay *prep. phr.*
indeed, 1454

fayerye *n.* fairyland, enchantment, 761

fayleth *v.3 sing.* fails, 452

fayn *adj.* pleased, keen, interested in,
146, 972

feble *adj.* feeble, 861

feblely *adv.* faintly, 1659

fecchen *v.* fetch, 450

fecht *n.* fight, 2042

feder *n.* feather

feint *adj.* faint, 2074

feire *adj.* fair, fine, 566

feith *n.* faith, 2297 in feith *adv. phr.*
indeed, 167, 473

felawschip, felawship *n.* fellowship,
friendship, 480, 1798

fele *v.* feel, 2695 feled *v. pt.* felt, 517
felte *v. pt.* felt, 326

ferde¹ *n.* fear, 1201

ferde² *pp.* gone, 796

fere¹ *n.* fear, 55, 437, 497

fere² *n.* companion, 2079, 2773

fere³ *adv.* far, 38, 931 ferer *adv.* farther,
2426n

ferly *n.* marvel, 761; *adj.* wondrous,
3033

fersly *adv.* fiercely, 237, 631

ferst *adj.* first, 2409

fey *adj.* fated, doomed, 1668

feynt *v.* faint, 2334

fiers *adj.* fierce, 2087

fifte *num. adj.* fifth, 610

fige *n.* fig, 1457

figure *n.* figure, dance movement, 2409

filosophres *n. pl.* philosophers,
alchemists, 961

fin¹ *n.* end, 620, 750

fin² *n.* fin, 1191 finnes *n. pl.* fins, 2329

fireherth *n.* fireplace, hearth, 848

fissch *n.* fish, 1182

fit *n.* misfortune, 2981 fits *n. pl.*
mishaps, 2982

fitt *n.* section of poetry

fitte *v.* fit, 156

flang *v. pt.* flung, 1801

flap *n.* slap, blow, 125; *v.* strike, 1628

flat *adv.* promptly, 1712

flatlinge *adv.* flat, 741

fleme *v.* chase, cause to flee, 1172

fleynge *pres. part.* flying, 1332

flien *v.* fly, 2039

flindermus *n.* bat (*moth-mouse*), 114

flore *n.* floor, 887

flotred *pp.* fluttered, 3014

floures *n. pl.* flowers, 161, 372

fly *n.* fly, insect, 1012

fnorteth *v.3 sing.* snores, snorts, 1341

fol[1] *n.* ignoramus; fool, 331

fol[2] *adj.* full, 3048

folie *n.* foolishness, 581, 762

foltisch *adj.* stupid, foolish, 9, 1204, 1763

folwen, folwe *v.* follow, 30, 486 folweth *v.3 sing.* 1423

for *conj.* because, 538, 2966

forfrigted *pp.* terrified, very frightened, 1071

forgite *v.* forget, 198

for-olde *adj.* very old, ancient, 2274

fors[1] *n.* matter, 67

fors[2] *n.* force, 1032

forschrank *v. pt.* dwindled away, 367

forsooth *adv.* in truth, indeed, 350, 511

forstolen *pp.* purloined, 2673

forther *adj.* further, additional, 489

forthest *adv.* farthest, 1066

forthynk *v.* regret, dismiss (an idea), 186 forthinketh *v.3 sing.* 2426i

Fortune *n.* Fortune; the goddess Fortuna, 567

forwes *n. pl.* furrows, 1938

foryete *v.* forget, 2104; *pp.* fogotten, 2101

foryeve *v.* forgive, 427

fostred *pp.* brought up, nurtured, 481

fot-hot *adv.* hotfoot, swift, 1179, 1327

foule *adj.* ugly, 2112

founteyns *n. pl.* fountains, 1780

fourme *n.* form, shape, 591

fournys *n.* furnace, 908

fox *n.* fox, 240

Fraunce *n.* France, 385

fray *n.* rumpus, terror, 878

free, fre *adj.* free, uncaged, 2604; liberal, 640

freke *n.* fellow, person, 2546c

Frensche of Stratford-atte-Bowe *n.* Anglo-Norman French, as spoken in London, not Parisian French, 416

freonden *v.* befriend, 1603

frete *v.* (*used of animals*) devour, 644 freted *pp.* devoured, 190 freteth *v.3 sing.* devours, 348h

fro *prep.* from, 1066

frogge *n.* frog, 1186

froske *n.* frog, 513

frouncing, frouning *pres.part.* frowning, 506, 2800 frouned *v. pt.* frowned, 632

frount *n.* front; forehead, 506

ful *adv.* fully, very, 21, 598

furre[1] *n.* fur, 476, 669

furre[2] *adj.* furry, 606a

fyne, fyn *adj.* fine, of high quality, 205, 2564c

fynt *v.3 sing.* (*contraction of* fyndeth) finds, 693, 2697

fyr *n.* fire, 195, 288, 433

fyrettes *n. pl.* ferrets, 671

gadred *v. pt.* gathered, 474

galonte *n.* person of fashion; a gallant, 309

galouns *n. pl.* gallons, 304

game *n.* game, fun, 2594

gamnede *v. pt.* played, 2546a

gan[1] *v.* began, 588; *auxiliary with infinitive indicating continuous action*, 23, 559

gan[2] *pp.* gone, 2814

gaped *v. pt.* yawned, gaped, 1055 gaping *pres. part.* yawning, 1651

gardineres *n. pl.* gardeners, 1783

gase *n.* gaze, staring, 2281

gat *v.* got, was given, 845

gaye *adj.* gay; cheerful, colourful, 469

gayne *v.* gain, get, 1973

geaunts *n. pl.* giants, 744

geli-fisch *n.* jellyfish, 2389

gentil *adj.* noble, well-born; kindly, 358

gentilly *adv.* in kindly fashion, 430

geomerie *n.* lamentation, 2315

geometre *n.* geometry, 80

geste *n.* jest, 2994

gestes *n. pl.* guests, 2194, 3052

gilti *adj.* guilty, 2933

ginneth *v.3 sing.* begins, 2594

gladdeth *v.3 sing.* gladdens, 2763

glasi *adj.* glassy, made of glass, 681

gle *n.* glee, delight, 716

glefully *adv.* gleefully, triumphantly, 2978

glent[1] *v. pt.* slipped, glided, 1754

glent[2] *v. pt.* glanced, looked, 1790

glode *v. pt.* glided, 121

goon[1] *v.* go, 163

goon[2] *pp.* gone, 38

gos *n.* goose, 813

gotous *adj.* gouty, 1358

goukes *n. pl.* cuckoos; fools 2619

governaunce *n.* behaviour, 1439; rule, authority, 491

gowk *n.* cuckoo, fool, 2324

grace *n.* grace, favour, 480, 505

grame *n.* annoyance, 2038

gramer *n.* grammar, 80

gramercy *adv.* thanks, 2415

gras[1] *n.* grace, 1800

gras[2] *n.* grass, 372, 1058

gren *v.* grin, 1466 (*also* **grinne**)

grennung, grennyng *verbal n.* grinning, 1463, 1972

gret *v. pt.* greeted, 2102

grete *adj.* great, 288

greves *n. pl.* groves, 1088

greveth *v.3 sing.* grieves, hurts, 410

grille *v.* irritate, anger, 1428

grinne *v.* grin, 1264 (*also* **gren**)

gripe *v.* seize, grip, 1345

grisly *adv.* very seriously, terribly, 2802

gristbitunge *n.* gnashing, 2343

groined *v. pt.* grunted, 2264

gronyng *verbal n.* groaning, 2255

grucche *v.* complain, 1788

gruf *adv.* prostrate, 1819

grylly *adv.* horribly, 1316a

Guillaume *n.* William, 417, 502a

gylden *adj.* golden, 148, 293

gyse *n.* manner, 912

haberdashere *n.* hatter, 1414

hacchen *v.* hatch, 1113

hadet *pp.* beheaded, 1815, 1897

haf *v.* have, 2974

haileth *v.3 sing.* salutes, greets, comes from, 1271

haire *n.* hair, 437 (*also* **heyre**)

hakke *v.* hack, chop, 1306

hals *n.* neck, 921, 1949

halvendel *n.* half, half part, 864

ham(ward) *adv.* home(ward), 384, 650

hap[1] *n.* happening, event, fortune, 671 **in hap** *prep. phr.* in case, 2742

hap[2] *v.* happen, 259, 707

harde *v. pt.* heard, 2142

hardinesse *n.* resolution, bravery, 892

hardly *adv.* scarcely, with difficulty, 370

haselwode *n.* hazel-wood (*used to express decided negative*), 794, 1131

hast *n.* haste, 129, 306

hasted *v. pt.* hastened, 2378

hastyflye *adv.* hastily, 445, 1036

hat *n.* hat, 1586 **my hat to borwe** *adv. phr.* I'd wager my hat (*strong assertion*), 692

hatte *pp.* was called, 1386

Hawes *n.* Stephen Hawes, 15th cent. poet, 556

hed *n.* head, 907 **heddes** *n. pl.* heads, 355

heddyng *verbal n.* beheading, 1967, 2218

hede *n.* heed, notice, 1504

hedlinge *adv.* headlong, 42

heere[1]*, here* *v.* hear, 82, 346, 515

heere[2]*, here* *adv.* here, 49, 1193

heft *v. pt.* lifted, heaved, 1044

hegge *n.* hedge, 32, 855

heires *n. pl.* hairs, whiskers, 669

helde *v. pt.* held, 489; regarded, 772

hele *n.* heel, 286 **heles** *n. pl.* 921

hem *pr.* them, 268, 479, 526

hem! *interj.* hum! ahem!, 499

hende *adj.* noble, honourable, polite, 246, 1510, 2942 **hendy** *adj.*1621

hepe *n.* heap, 126; a lot, a great deal, 352

heraud *n.* herald, 2641

herbes *n. pl.* plants, 1062

here *see* **heere**; *see* **heyre**

heres *n. pl.* hairs, 135, 1472

herkneth *v. imper.pl.* herken, listen, 493, 500

herne *n.* corner, 134, 1490, 2842

hertes *n. pl.* hearts, 1830

herthe *n.* hearth, 1265

heste, hest *n.* bihest, bidding, 714, 1308

hete *v.* command, 1942

heve *v.* raise, heave, 1075

heved *n.* head, 2965

hevedling *adv.* headfirst, 2761
hevie *adj.* burdensome, 516e
hevinesse *n.* misery, 668
hewe *n.* hue, 1782
heyre, here *n.* hair, 2526b, 3039
hi *adv.* high, 1926
hie¹ *n.* haste, 2712
hie² *adv.* high 373, 467
high *adv.* high, 273
highte *n.* height, 259, 291, 366
hine *n.* servant, peasant, 821
hir¹, hire *pr.* her (*obj.*), 1909; herself, 3011; *posses.*, 648, 1962 **hir thought** *v. phr.* it seemed to her, she thought, 266
hir² *adj.* their, 480 **hires** *poss. pr.* theirs, 587
hirself *pr.* herself, 569
his *adj.* his, 508e; its, 520, 909
historie *n.* history, personal story, 593
holy days, *n. pl.* holidays (*church festival days, when saints were commemorated*), 2170
honestly *adv.* honourably, appropriately, usefully, 1584
honie *n.* honey, 2098
honour *n.* honour, respect, 1396
hool *adj.* whole, 785; healthy, 1678
hoold, hold *v.* hold, stop, 549; consider, 2108 **hold faste** *v. phr.* hold firm, pay attention, 508
hooli *adv.* wholly, 128
hope¹ *n.* hope, 297; *v.* hope, 109
hope² *v.* expect, 2605, 2902
hors¹ *n.* horse, 68, 923
hors² *adj.* hoarse, 348
hoses *n. pl.* stockings, 278
houling *pres. part.* howling, 1263
hous *n.* house, 986
houskepare *n.* housekeeper, 690
Hous of Fame *n.* Chaucer's poem *The House of Fame* (*in which see lines* 730-41), 60
hoved *v. pt.* lingered, 750
hoveth *v. impers.* it behoves (you), you ought, 299, 2797
hrafen *n.* raven, 1513
huf! *interj.* exclamation of pride, 309
hurchouns *n. pl.* hedgehogs, 1939
hurlen *v.* hurl, 2400

hus *n.* house, 448
hwiles *conj.* while, 691
Ierusalem *n.* Jerusalem, 388
ill *adj.* bad, 1698
imperial *adj.* imperial, majestic
import *n.* subject, concern, 478, 1008
importeth *v. 3 sing.* implies, means, matters, 1563, 2866
impossible *n.* impossibility, 364
incres *n.* increase, 1747
indicatyf *adj.* indicating, 561
inditen *v.* write, 2880
inquisitif *adj.* inquisitive, 413
instanter adv. (*Latin*) immediately, vehemently, 2675
intentyflye *adv.* intently, 934, 2000
interen, intren *v.* enter, 213, 224
interyng *verbal n.* entering, getting in, 297
irchoun, irchon *n.* hedgehog, 1950, 2756
ire *n.* anger, 427, 477
iren toles *n. pl.* iron tools, fireirons, 1288
irous *adj.* angry, 611
iuree , iure *n.* jury, 2609, 2970
iwis *adv.* certainly, indeed, 516c, 2730
janglyng *adj.* talkative, 647
jet *n.* fashion, 476
jewel *n.* jewel, thing of value, 579
jogged *v. pt.* jerked, 1789
joly *adj.* attractive, 448; happy, 348d
joye *n.* delight, 423
juge *v.* judge, propose, 521; *n.* judge, 606i
juparde *n.* jeopardy, danger, 924
jurre *n.* jury, 606i
jururs *n. pl.* jurors, 2601
just *adj.* exact, 567
juste *v.* joust, 184
keep *n.* notice, 430; *v.* keep, control, 2289 **took no keep** *v. phr.* did not bother, 2023
kei¹ *n.* key, 148; **key** *n.* 374
kei² *n.* quay, 380
kens *v.3 sing.* (*Northern*) knows, 812
ketel *n.* cauldron, pot, kettle, 1216, 1257
kevered *pp.* covered, 2440; recovered, 2855
kicchene, kicchen *n.* kitchen, 1255, 2085

kicke *v.* kick, 848 **kicked** *v. pt.* kicked, 853

kidz *n. posses. pl.* kids', 311

kiked *v. pt.* looked, gazed, 1205, 2861

kinde *n.* kind, kindred (*of the same nature, sort*), 2141

kitte *v.* cut, 197 **kittyng** *verbal n.* cutting, 1504

klokke *n.* clock, 1605

kne *n.* knee, 2751, 2960

knele *v.* kneel, 739

knewe I but *v. phr.* if only I knew, 171

knokked *v. pt.* knocked, 699, 1183

knokles *n. pl.* knuckles, 1183

knyff *n.* knife, 1552

kyndely *adj.* natural, 61

kynes *n. posses.* kine's; of cattle, 3071

lacche *v.* catch, seize, 2426h

lahter *n.* laughter, 1928, 3000

laiked *v. pt.* played, 2526c

lak *n.* lack, 1587, 1684; *v.* be without, 176, 620

lake *n.* lake, 270

lampreis *n. pl.* lampreys (*fish with a sucker-like mouth*), 2426c

lang *adj.* long, 837

Langland 14th-century author of the dream vision poem Piers Plowman

lardid *pp.* larded, greased, 2526a

last[1] *n.* burden, 375

last[2], **laste** *n.* last, 484, 517

lat *v.* let, 346 **lat slyde** *v. pt.* let go, ignored, 272

latte *v. pt.* let, caused, 3056

Latyn *n.* Latin, 407

launce *v.* launch, fling, 2426h

leche *n.* leech, surgeon, 1026ee

led[1] *v. pt.* led, 130, 1766; *pp.* 2920

led[2] *n.* lead, caldron, 908

leed *n.* lead, 2752

leefe, lefe *n.* leaf, 214, 935

leeve[1], **leve** *v.* believe, 525, 1516

leeve[2] *v.* leave, 721

legend *n.* inscription, writing, 723

leiser *n.* leisure, 1606

lele *adj.* loyal; suitable, 285

leme *n.* flame, 221

lencthe *n.* length, height, 212, 902

lened *v. pt.* leaned, 933

lenger *adv.* longer, 2166

lepes *n. pl.* leaps, leaping, 2402

lerde *v. pt.* learnt, 2334

lere *v.* learn, 1424 **lered** *v. pt.* learnt, 419

lerne *v.* learn, 386

lesarde *n.* lizard, 896, 2637

lesse *adv.* less, smaller, 365

leste *v. pt.* wished to, 635; *v.* wishes to, 1194

lesyng *verbal n.* lying, telling lies, 1322d

let[1] *pp.* prevented 1026u **letteth** *v. 3 sing.* hinders, blocks, 1554

let[2] *v.* allow, permit, 1574

lettres *n. pl.* letters, 285

leve[1] *v.* leave, 2700

leve[2] *v.* believe, 1516

lever *adv.* rather, 630, 1040

leyser *n.* leisure

licour *n.* liquid, 1053

liggyng *pres.part.* lying, 2220, 3011

lik *adj.* likely, 2001

liketh *v. impers.* likes **me liketh** *v. phr.* it pleases me, I like, 358 **as liked hem** *adv. phr.* as they pleased, 545

lime, lim *n.* limb, table leg, 230, 1464

limpeth *v.3 sing.* happens, 2121

ling *n.* ling (*a cod-like fish*), 2387

lippes *n. pl.* lips, 1076

liquor *n.* liquid, drink, 205

liste[1] *n.* edge of garment, 2829

liste[2] *v.* wanted to, 488

listeth *v. imper.* listen

litargie *n.* lethargy, 2316

lite *n.* little, 332

liveree *n.* livery, servant's uniform, 1181

livynge *pres. part.* living, who live, 388

locus amoenus *n.* (*Latin*) "delightful place" i.e. Eden, the earthly paradise, 162

lofte *n.* loft, upper room or region **on lofte** *adv. phr.* aloft, on high, 2764

logge *v.* lodge, 2312

lok[1] *n.* lock, 155 **lokkes** *n. pl.* locks, 150

lok[2] *v.* look, 817 **loke** *v.* look, 45, 187

loked *v. pt.* looked, 413, 3037

lokked *pp.* locked, 141

lokunge bras *n.* reflecting brass, looking-glass, mirror, 722

looth *adj.* unwilling, 2360 (*also* **loth**)

lopstere *n.* lobster, 2377

lore *n.* teaching, 2270

lose *adj.* loose, 840

losel *n.* lazy rogue, 804

loth *adj.* unwilling 314, 515, hating, 465

loude *adv.* loudly, 425, 580

lough *v.* laugh, 582; *v. pt.* laughed, 527

louted *v. pt.* bowed, bent, 2750

loweth *v.3 sing.* lows, 348f

lowynge *verbal n.* lowing, 3071

lufly[1] *adj.* lovely, beautiful, 183

lufly[2] *adv.* lovingly, 2081

lully lully *n.* lullaby sounds, 1315

lust *n.* desire, 568

luven *v.* love, 446

luxure *n.* enjoyment, 1016

lyf *n.* life, 262 **on lyf** *prep. phr.* alive, 371 **on lyve** alive, 64

lyflode *n.* sustinence, 1672

lyft *adj.* left, left side, 1078, 1416

madde, mad *v.* am/are mad, 602, 2960

magik naturel *n.* good (*i.e.* benign) magic (*natural consequence as opposed to demonic miracle*), 749

magyk *adj.* magic, 886

maillet *n.* mallet, 2038 **maillets** *n. pl.*, 1940

maister *n.* master, teacher, 491, 555

maistresse *n.* mistress, madam, 1811

makyng *n.* poetic composition, 768

male *n.* bag, 23, 566, 2500

malencholie *adj.* melancholy, 2850

man *n.* someone, one, man, 28, 260

maner *n.* manner, 499, 540

mansionyng *n.* station (*one of equal divisions of a planet's motions across the sky*), 1304

mantel *n.* mantle, cape, 709

mappamoundes *n. pl.* maps of the world, *mappaemundi*, 50

marchaunts *n. pl.* merchants, 381

Marie! *interj.* (by) Mary!, 459

Mars *n.* the planet Mars, 1304

mat *adj.* tired, 2, 661

matiere *n.* (*French*) material content, 1570

matins *n.* early morning church service, 2352

maugre *prep.* despite, 988 **maugre Alys cheke** *prep. phr.* in spite of Alice, 1108

maw *n.* stomach, inside, 2560

mea culpa *n.* (*Latin*) I'm sorry; my fault, 422, 438, 609

mede *n.* mead (*fermented honey drink*), 348c

medes *n. pl.* meadows, 3066

mein *n.* strength, 596

menestow *v.2 sing.* (menest + thou) do you mean, 973 **meneth** *v.3 sing.* means, 511, 1593

menged *pp.* mixed, mingled, 204, 3058

Mercia *n.* Mercia (*central England in Old English times*), 502f

merke *v.* mark out, 541 **merked** *pp.* marked, 199

merkst *v. 2 sing.* mark, attend to, 607

merveille *v.* marvel, am amazed, 1270

merveillous *adj.* marvellous, 1082

messagere, messager *n.* messenger, 284, 703

meschaunce *n.* misfortune, 1150

mesure *n.* size, 890 **mesures** *n. pl.* sizes, 982

met[1] *v. pt.* met, 428, 702

met[2] *v. pt.* dreamed, 121, 3035

mete *v.* measure, 365

methinketh *v. 3 sing. impers.* it seems to me, I think, 92, 325

methought *v. pt. impers.* it seemed to me, I thought, 508, 610

mevyng *verbal n.* moving, 1086

meynie *n.* company, 580

mi *adj.* my, 713

middelerth *n.* the earth, regarded as in the middle of the concentric spheres on which the planets and the fixed stars revolve, and also as midway between Heaven and Hell, 74

might *n.* strength, 829

mihti *adj.* mighty, 502g

miladi *pr.* Madam, my lady, 97, 708

min *pr.* mine, 330 **mine** *adj.* my, 1578

minne *v.* remind, 1306; remember, 1727 **me minne** remind myself, remember, 75

minstrelcye *n.* musical performance, concert, 1619

mirie *adj.* merry, 2994

mis *v.* miss, fail to hear, 605

mise *n. pl.* mice, 112, 410 (*also* mys)

misst *pp.* missed, 2031

mister *n.* trade, occupation, 2276

mo *adj.* more, 202, 2882

mode *n.* mood, emotion, 2182

modres *n. poss.* mother's, 632

mokke *adj.* mock, imitation, 2208

mone *n.* moon, 868

monie *adj.* many, 502d

monkes *n. pl.* monks, 388

moot *v.* must, 73, 284, 569

mordereth *v.3 sing.* is murdering, 1632

mordre *n.* murder, 1353

mors marine *n.* morse, walrus, sea-horse, 2388

morwenyng *n.* morning, 324

moste, most *v.* must 558, 739

moteryng *pres. part.* muttering, 312, 667

motlee *adj.* varicoloured, diverse, 563

mous-falles *n. pl.* mouse-traps, 1745

mow *v.* might, 1151

mowe *n.* pursing of the lips, frown, face (*as pulled*), 2870

mucilage *n.* viscous fluid, mucus, 2315

multiplicatioun *n.* multiplication, 341

mus *n.* mouse, 265, 401

mused *v. pt.* mused, thought, 7, 1439

mushole *n.* mouse-hole, 711

musseroun *n.* mushroom, 943

mynd *n.* mind, 7

myrie *adv.* merrily, 348g

mys *n. pl.* mice, 436

nadde *v. pt.* (ne + had) had not, 5, 297, 391

nam *v.* (ne + am) am not, 329, 633

namoore *n.* no more, 484, 1582, 2936

narwe *adj.* narrow, confined, 351, 848

nas *v. pt.* (ne + was) was not, 15, 65

natandi verbal n. (*Latin*) of swimming, 409

natheles, nathles *adv.* none the less, nevertheless, 302, 389 nathelesse,723

naught *n.* nought, nothing, 2532

nawhit *adv.* not at all, 614

nayther *conj.* neither, 1418

ne *conj.* nor, 2167; *adv.* not 2192 ne … ne *conj.* neither … nor, 6

nebors *n. posses.* neighbour's, 2628

nedes most *adv. phr.* needs must, necessarily, (I shall) have to, 95

nei wat *adv.* all but, 1316, 1741

nek *n.* neck, 1026y

ner *adv.* nearer, 397

nere *v. pt.* (ne + were) was not, 376

nese *n.* nose, 1026aa; *v.* sneeze, 3054

nesing *verbal n.* sneezing, 1214, 3068; *pres. part.* 1259

netes *n. posses.* ox's netes skin *n.* leather, 2760

neveradel *adv.* not at all (*lit.* never a bit), 847

newefangel *adj.* novel, newfangled, 2330

nice *adj.* exact, in fact, 508f

nigardlye *adj.* stingy, 2100

nigh *adv.* near, 274

nighen *num.* nine, 2520

nik *n.* nick, cut, 1026y

nikked *v. pt.* (ne + ik, not I) said not nikked him nay *v. phr.* assured him 'No', 508, 1616

nil *v.* (ne + wil) will not, 1635

nilly *v.* (ne + will + he) he will not, 1602

nis *v.* (ne + is) is not, 1699

niste *v. pt.* (ne + wiste) did not know, 63

nithe *prep.* beneath, under, 2720

nobbut *adv.* nothing but, 1094

nobles *n. pl.* noblemen, 502d

nois *n.* noise, sound, 805 (*also* noys)

nolde *v. pt.* (ne + wolde) did not want to, would not, 55, 483

nole *v.* (ne + wol) don't want to, 439

none *n.* noon, 369

nones *n.* for the nones (= for the (n)once) for the occasion, very (*tag of little meaning*), 522, 686

noon[1] *n.* noon, 1609

noon[2] *pr.* (ne + oon) not one, none, 2091

noot *v.* (ne + woot) do not know, 524

norice *n.* nurse, 710, 2127

norisse *v.* nurse, nourish, 435

Normandie *n.* Normandy, 417, 502a

Northumbria *n.* Northumbria, 502g

nosethirles *n. pl.* nostrils, 136

not¹ *adv.* not, 329, 2735

not² *v.* (ne + **wot**) do not know, 320, 1037

noted *v. pt.* took notice of, 952

nother *adj.* neither, 119, 2281

nourisschen *v.* nurse, nourish, 1314

noyaunce *n.* annoyance, 1117

noys *n.* noise, 1212, 2766

of¹ *adv.* off, away, 275, 293, 458, 1114

of² *prep.* for, 505

oferloken *v.* look over, 2878

ofer-more *adv.* moreover, 2888

ofersetting *verbal n.* upsetting, being turned upside-down, 2856

offenden *v.* offend, 596

ofshere *v.* slice off, 1296

oft *adv.* often, 1952

oftake *v.* take off, remove, 1316

oistre *n.* oyster, 634

ony *adj.* any, 454, 496

onys *adv.* once, 239, 382 **at ones** *adv. phr.* immediately, 521, 685

oone, oon, one, on *pr.* one, 646 **at oon** *adv. phr.* all together, 2791

ooth *n.* oath, 1578

ope *v.* open, 149 **oped** *v. pt.* opened, 157

orbis terrarum *n.(Latin)* the earth, 336

otia n. (*Latin*) idleness, leisure, 1606

où est ma chatte *n. phr.* (*French*) where is my cat? (*first sentence in La Baga-telle, a child's French grammar*), 419

ought *n.* anything, 513

oure *pr.* ours, 2303

oute, alas! *interj.* Oh dear!, 360

outrely *adv.* utterly, 680

outtake, outake *prep.* except, 1558 **outake a cat dyde grinne** except for a cat that grinned, 1264

overall *adv.* entirely, 164

over more *adv.* moreover, 525

overset *v.* upset, overturn, 2831

over thwert *prep.* across, 2367

owest *v. 2 sing.* ought, 1508

oweth *v. 3 sing.* owns, 453

Oxenford *n.* Oxford (*university city where Lewis Carroll and Alice Liddell lived*), 1389

paire *n.* pair, 720

pakke *n.* pack, 1860, 3007

pan *n.* head, 526

pannes *n. pl.* vessels, pans, 1289

papengaye *n.* parrot, 470, 483

par by (*French*) **par aventure** *adv.* by chance, 915, 1015 **pardee** *adv.* (by God) indeed, 291 **par (ma) fey** *adv.* indeed, by my faith, 156, 333, 649

paradise *n.* beautiful garden, paradise, 903

parcenere *n.* partner, 2392

parchemayn *n.* parchment (*sheep's or goat's skin prepared as writing material*), 2583

pardee *see* par

pare *v.* prepare, 3050

parfay *see* par

parlement *n.* discussion, 478, 521

parti *n.* company, 543

pas *n.* situation, 809

pasties *n. pl.* pies, pastries, 1026o

pasud *v. pt.* passed, went, 2544

patron *n.* pattern, 1865

paw *n.* paw, 910 **pawes** *n. pl.* paws, 2319

paye *n.* pleasing **to paye** *prep.phr.* pleasing 12, 1279

pece *n.* piece, 255, 2687

pedlers *n. posses.* pedlar's, 169

pees *n.* quiet, peace; *as interj.* be quiet!, 1313

pegges *n. pl.* pegs, 50

peine *n.* pains, great effort, 35, 642

peinture *n.* painting, picture, 4, 2222 **peintures** *n. pl.* pictures, 1864

peires *n. pl.* pairs, 719

pelet *n.* pellet, pebble, 2893

pell-mell *n.* pall mall (*a game with ball and mallet resembling croquet*), 1195

pens *n.* pence, 2671, 2951

peped *v. pt.* peeped, 1203

peper *n.* pepper, 1258 (*also* piper)

per cas *adv.* perhaps, 170, 399

peraventure *adv.* by chance, 802

perchance *adv.* perhaps, 98

perforce *adv.* by force, 739

perned *v. pt.* preened, 2546b

persawe *v. pt.* perceived, 389, 885

perseverance *n.* perseverance, determination, 2012

persevered *v. pt.* continued, persevered, 2539

personeles *adj.* personal (*plural with 'sawes'*), 1509, 1691

pertourbed *pp.* perturbed, worried, 1359

pertriche *n.* partridge, 2546b

pese, pes *n.* peace; *as interj.* be quiet!, 500, 1752

peyneth *v.3 sing.* pains, troubles, 1117

Phoenix *n.* Phoenix (*fabled unique bird that resurrects itself from its own funeral pyre*), 470

pighte, *pp.* stuck, 77; *v. pt.* thrust, 1772

pilgrymage *n.* pilgrimage, 2482

pipe *v.* pipe, squeak **how hard hit pipe** *adv. phr.* no matter how hard it might squeak, 1346

piper *n.* pepper, 2804 **piper box** *n.* pepper shaker, 2789

piren *v.* peer, 3, 296 **pired** *v. pt.* peered, 948, 1917

pise *n.* pea, 1026n

plank *n.* plank, wooden floor, 368

plasche *n.* splash, 377 **plaschinge** *verbal n.* splashing, 397

plat *adv.* flat, plain, at once, 1518

plate *n.* (door)plate, 698

platter *n.* plate, 1234 **platters** *n. pl.*, 1289

playe *n.* play, (of) playing, 540; *v.* play, 582 (*also* **pleyen**)

plentevously *adv.* abundantly, 392

plete *v.* complain, 586, 617

pletyng *verbal n.* pleading, 1046

pleyen *v.* play, 910

pleyn *adj.* plain, clear, 60 **pleyner** *adj.* plainer, clearer, 980

plounged *v. pt.* plunged, 1557

plukke *v.* pluck, 11

poesie *n.* poetry, 2515

pol[1] *n.* pool, 268, 389

pol[2] *n.* head, 776

Pope *n.* Pope, 502b

pore *adj.* poor, 660, 845

porpeis *n.* porpoise, 2426b

pose[1] *n.* head cold, 498

pose[2] *v.* suggest, propose, 1652

poudred *pp.* powdered, 1188

povre *adj.* poor, unfortunate, 1369; impecunious, 2724; incapable, 2755

poynt *n.* point(ing at), 561

poynting *pres. part.* pointing, indicating, 556

poysoun *n.* poison, 1678

praunce *v.* prance, 2554

praye *v. imper.* please, I beg, 97

presse *n.* cupboard, 57 **presses** *n. pl.*, 49

Prester John *n.* Prester John (*fabled Christian ruler in the mysterious East*), 98

pretenden *v.* pretend, 243

prettie *adj.* pretty, 2413

preve *v.* prove (to be), 1026ee **preved** *v. pt.* proved, followed logically, 1424

priked *v. pt.* pricked, incited, 2347

prime *n.* first hour of the day, often 6 a.m., 1607

prise *n.* prize, 558

prithee *adv.* please ([I] pray thee), 1402

prive *adj.* privy, secret **prive roum** secret room (*pun on "trivium"*), 2310

proces *n.* process, procedure, 516g, 2775; narrative, written passage, 2913

proferen *v.* put forward, offer, 1507 **profred** *v. pt.* offered, 577

propre *adj.* (one's) own, proper, 902, 1160, 2842

protestacioun *n.* protest, 1124

pryde *n.* pride, 516f

pucelles *n. pl.* young girls, 2608

punisched *pp.* punished, 394

purgatorye *n.* Purgatory (*place of future punishment*), 1322b

purpre *adj.* purple, 3002

purvei *v.* make arrangements for, manage, 905 **purveyde** *pp.* provided, ready, 612

putte *n.* shotput, putting the stone, 242

pye *n.* magpie, 647

pyp *n.* pipe, 958, 988

quaad *adj.* bad **quaad last** *n.* heavy burden, 375 **Quaad Lyvyng Toun** *n.* bad living town (*pun on "quadrivium"*), 2313

quarterne *n.* prison, 36

queise *v.* squeeze, 2702

quelle *v.* kill, 55, 456

queme *v.* please, 276

quencht *v. pt.* quenched, suppressed, 1012

quere, quer *n.* chorus, choir, 559, 854

querele *n.* quarrel, 1616; trial, 2567; *v.* quarrel, 1988

quicke *adj.* alive, 1992 (*also* quyk)

quikened *v. pt.* came alive, 3042

quille *n.* quill, feather, pen (*bird's feather used as a pen*), 1590

quod *v. pt.* quoth, said, 181, 873

quyk *adj.* alive, 820

rachetehes *n. pl.* chains, 2581

radly *adv.* eagerly, 456

rafters *n. pl.* roof beams, 1318

rap¹ *n.* blow, 1622, 1966

rap² *n.* rope, 2760

ratelen *v.* rattle, 3048 ratelyng *pres. part.* rattling, 3066 ratled *v. pt.* rattled, 879

ratouns *n. posses.* rat's, 158

rattes *n. pl.* rats, 456

rau *adj.* raw, 1149

raughte, raught *pp.* reached, seized, 194, 1946; expounded, told, 2344

rave *v.* rave, go mad, 2860

rawe *n.* row, 1938

real *adj.* regal, 499

recchen *v.* reach. 227, 274, 279, 836 recched *pp.* reached, 750

reche *v.* reach, 274, 936 recheth *v.3 sing.* reaches, 1665

recto *n.* right side (*of a page*), 2910

red¹ *adj.* red, 13; red-faced with anger, 1631

red², redde *v. pt.* read (*past tense*), 4, 189 redde no texte *v. phr.* could not see, 46

redeth *v. imper. pl.* read, 265; *polite pl.* 2641

redily *adv.* promptly, 1566

reduced *pp.* brought back, adapted

reedi *adj.* reed-strewn, 287

reguler *adj.* regular, according to rule, legal, 2889

reherse *v.* repeat, 1025

reisins *n. pl.* raisins. 250

rekenen *v.* reckon, enumerate, 2431

relefe *n.* relief, 2301

releved *pp.* relieved, 2815

remayne, remayn *v.* remain, stay, 353, 617

remedee *n.* remedy, 2022 remedies *n. pl.* remedies, 522

remue *v.* remove, 2451

ren *v.* run, 92

render *v.* render, translate, 2669

renne *v.* run, 529, 643 rennynge, rennyng *pres. part.*, 2372, 2991 rennyng *verbal n.*, 545

repere *v.* go (repair), 652

repeted *v. pt.* repeated, 1103

requireth *v.3 sing.* requires, is asking for, 1690

rerde *n.* noise, 661

reremous *n.* bat, 113

reresouper *n.* after (back, rear) supper, extra meal, *ch. VII title*

rescoue *v.* rescue, 1350

rese *n.* rush, race, 546

resten *v.* rest, 934

reulen *v.* give instructions, 177

reverence *n.* respect, 2011

rewle *n.* rule, requirement, 1844

reyn *n.* rain, 2990

rhethorique *n.* speech, composition, 336

ridels *n. pl.* riddles, 1515

rigges *n. pl.* ridges, 1938

rine *v.* touch, 822

ripelen *v.* ripple, 3065

ris *n.* spray, twig, 1582

robyshe *n.* rubbish, 2531

rode *n.* red complexion, face, 1873

rof *n.* roof, ceiling, 140, 839, 2861

rof-tile *n.* tile from the roof, 1624b

rogh, rough *adj.* rough, 541, 1938

rokke¹ *n.* rock, 2243

rokke² *v.* rock, 1323

Roma capud n. (*Latin*) Rome the capital, 343

romaunce *n.* romance, tale of wonder, 763

rombling *verbal n.* rumbling, 830

roote, root, rote, rot *n.* root, 204 rotes *n. pl.* roots, 1107

rored *v. pt.* roared, 1910

ros *v. pt.* rose, stood up, 519

roser *n.* rose-bush, 1782

roten *pp.* rotten, questionable, 2526d
rough *see* **rogh**
roum *n.* room, 888, 1327, 1490
roun *v.* whisper, chat, 867
routeth *v. 3 sing.* snores, snorts, 2265
rowe *n.* row, line, 1938, 2896
russhe *n.* rush, reed,767
russled *v. pt.* rustled, 3045
rutelen *v.* rustle, 3064
sa *adv.* (*Northern*) so, 815
sadde *adj.* sad, 598, 601
sage *adj.* wise, clever, 1720
sahtled *v. pt.* made peace, 502c
sak *n.* bag, pocket, 1775
salten *adj.* salty, 378
sam *adv.* together, 502c
sans doute *prep. phr.* without doubt,
   415, 1909
sauf *adj.* safe, 745
saufloker *adv.* more safely, 2229
saufly *adv.* safely, 900
sauvage *adj.* savage, 1633, 2230
save *prep.* except, 2206
sawe *n.* saying, 1559 **sawes** *n. pl.*
   remarks, 1509, 1691
saystow *v. 2 sing.* (**sayest** + **thou**) do you
   say?, 601
scars *adj.* scarce, neglible, 776
scarsely, scarsly *adv.* scarcely, hardly,
   1629, 2525
schade *n.* shade, shadow, 2195
schame, scham *n.* shame, 299, 390
scheily *adv.* shyly, 967, 1392
schene *n.* shine, 2220
schephirde *n.* shepherd, 3068
schette *v. pt.* shut, 2894
schlates *n. pl.* slates, 2612
schlatestanes *n. pl.* slates (*lit.* slate
   stones), 2626
schoke, schok *v. pt.* shook, 1056, 2719
schole *n.* school, 2273
schore *n.* shore, 393, 464
schorte *adj.* short, 479 **schorter**, 1158
   schortlye *adv.* shortly, soon, 206
schowe *n.* soup, 2561
schraping *verbal n.* scraping, 850
schriched *v. pt.* screeched, 3004
schrille *adj.* shrill, 854

schrimpes *n. pl.* shrimps (*edible
   crustaceans, small and insignificant*),
   2471
schuldren, schuldres *n. pl.* shoulders,
   166, 1085
schutte *v.* shut, 210; *pp.* 241, 373
scrattin *v.* scratch, 851
scribes *n. posses.* writer's, copyist's, 1513
scriche *n.* screech, 799 **scriches** *n. pl.*
   823
script *n.* (hand)writing, 2914
scrowe *n.* scroll, 2583
se[1] *n.* sea, 379, 383
se[2] *v.* see, 12
seche *v.* seek, 451
secree *n.* secret, 2944w
sede *n.* seed, 348c
seestow *v.2 sing.* (**seest** + **thou**), you see
   171
seigh *v. pt.* saw, 1804, 2196
seined *pp.* signed, 2924; *v. pt.* 2925
Seint Jame *n.* Santiago de Compostella
   (*shrine of the Apostle James, in Spain*),
   387
Seinte Loy *n.* probably St. Eligius,
   patron saint of goldsmiths **by Seinte
   Loy** *prep.phr.* a very mild oath, 1322c
seke[1] *adj.* sick, 1677
seke[2] *v.* seek, 10
selde *adv.* seldom, 236, 1338
sele *n.* seal, 285
seles *n. pl.* seals (*the animals*), 2387
sellic *adv.* amazingly, wonderfully, 2711
sen *n.* (*French*) sense, meaning, 1571
sene *pp.* seen, 383
sens *n.* sense, 1726
se-ormista *n.* marine geography, 2231
servys *n.* service, 280
set *v. pt.* set, 155 **set me** *v.* determine,
   353
setled *v. pt.* settled, 1151
se-tortus *n.* turtle (*sea-tortoise*), 2208
seydestow *v. pt.* (**seydest** + **thou**) did you
   say?, 1457
seyn, sey *v.* say, 59, 301
seynt *n.* saint, 556
shaltow *v.* (**shalt** + **thou**) you will, you
   must, 835
shapen *pp.* shaped, made, 2426o

shere *v.* shear, 2811
shippes *n. pl.* ships, 383
shires *n posses.* shire's, country's, 2426o
sho *n.* shoe, 1954
sholde *v.* should, would, 636
shoon, shoos *n.* shoes, 278, 284
shope *v. pt.* prepared (*lit.* shaped), 502d
shote *v.* shoot, 882
shoures *n. pl.* showers, 1312
showe *n.* show, display, 584
shrighte *v. pt.* shrieked, 1120
shrike[1] *n.* shriek, 1744
shrike[2] *v.* shriek, 1875 **shriked** *v. pt.*
   shrieked, yelled, 2407
shrynken *v.* shrink, 893
shuldre *n.* shoulder, 1560
shutte *adj.* shut, closed, 1742
siked *v. pt.* sighed, 626, 1547
si'l vous plait *prep. phr.* (*French*
   [*mocking the White Rabbit for aping the*
   upper classes who spoke Anglo-French])
   if you please, 1916
silly *adj.* innocent, foolish, 331
sith *adv.* since, ago, 1876
sitteth *v. imper.pl.* sit, 492
siyed *v.* sighed, 573, 597
skil *n.* skill, ability, 1383 **skile** *adj.*
   clever, 2095
skyes *n. pl.* clouds, 1622b
slak *adj.* slack, relaxed, 2194
slat *n.* slate, 840
slaye *v.* slay, kill, 924
sleighte *n.* skill, 1153
Sleuthe *n.* Sloth (*personified: see* Langland, *Piers Plowman*, B. v. 386), 2519
sliper *adj.* slippery, 230
sloggard *n.* sluggard, lazybones, 2223
sluggardly *adv.* lazily, sluggishly, 963
slyde *v.* slide, pass, go, 272
slymy *adj.* slimy, 2519
slypped *pp.* slipped, 398 **slypte** *v. pt.*
   slipped, 377
smal *adj.* small, little, 276
smere *v.* smear, spread, 1553
smiten *v.* strike, hit, 883
smoot *v. pt.* smote, 880
snacche *v.* snatch, grab 798, 822
   snacched *v. pt.* snatched, 2635
snaile *n.* snail, 2426a

snute *n.* snout, 1362
snybbed *v. pt.* rebuked, 1701
sobre *adj.* sober, solemn, 582
sobrely *adv.* gravely, 571
sodeyn *adj.* sudden, 549
sodeynly *adv.* suddenly, 14, 323, 377
softe *adv.* softly, 348b
soght *v. pt.* sought, went to, 372
sok *n.* sock, 2720
solas *n.* solace, comfort, 1654
sole *n.* sole of the foot, 440 **soles** *n. pl.*
   2469 (*also edible flat-fish*)
soleinly *adv.* morosely, sullenly, 1243
solempne *adj.* solemn, 584
solempnely *adv.* solemnly, with dignity,
   520
som[1] *adj.* some, a certain amount, 510
som[2] *n.* total, 339
somdel *adv.* somewhat, 93, 326
someres *n. pl.* summers, 3084
sone *adv.* soon, 370 **soner** *adv.* sooner,
   530
sooth *n.* truth, 124, 338
soothfastnesse *n.* truthfulness, 738
soote *adj.* sweet, 160, 585
sorhful *adj.* sorrowful, 438, 459, 518
sori *adj.* sorry, miserable, unfortunate,
   24, 809
soster *n.* sister, 2 **sostres** *n. pl.* sisters,
   1669
soudeurs *n. pl.* soldiers, 385, 1822
soun *n.* sound, 606
sounder *n.* litter **swynes [away] from the**
   sounder *n. pl.* pigs no longer piglets,
   897
souped *v. pt.* supped, 1482
souper *n.* supper, 1636, 3024
souple *adj.* supple, 1090
sourly *adv.* sullenly, morosely, 1150
sovereyne *adj.* sovereign, unfailing, 2022
space *n.* opportunity, time, 44, 479,
   2241
spak *v. pt.* spoke, 315, 2911
sparwes *n. pl.* sparrows, 1582
speche *n.* speech, 489
spectacle *n.* spectacles, 2623
spedest *v.2 sing.* succeed, do well, 1975
spekere *n.* speaker, 2755

spendeth *v.3 sing.* spends, uses, wastes, 2497

speres *n. pl.* spheres (*concentric spheres on which the planets and fixed stars were thought to revolve*), 1299

spicerie *n.* spices, 2097

spigot *n.* tap, 303

spilt *v. pt.* died, came to grief, 1324

spradde, spredde *v.* spread, 797, 822; *pp.* 2959

sprengen *v.* sprinkle, 1787

spye, spy *v.* espy, see, 136, 547

squeked *v. pt.* squeaked, 2631 **squekyng** *adj.* squeaking, 861

stad *pp.* settled, placed, stood, 1944

stal *v. pt.* stole, 2644c

stant *v.3 sing.* (**standeth**) stands, 1636

stare *n.* starling, 2936

stare *v.* stare, gaze fixedly, 2958

stayde *pp.* stayed, stopped, 1706

stayre *n.* stair(s), staircase, 67, 700

stedde *v. pt.* been placed, stood, 2591

stede, sted *n.* place, 62, 624 **stedes** *n. pl.*, 1932

steked *v. pt.* stuck, 2451

stem *v.* stem, stop, 2178

stemyng *adj.* steaming, 1257

ster *n.* star, 2275

stere *v.* steer, proceed, 516

sterre-fissh, ster-fissh *n.* starfish, 1340, 2273

sterk *adj.* strong, violent, 1616

sterted *v. pt.* jumped, was startled, 1273

sterven *v.* die, 2839

stewe *n.* stew, 1257

stif *adv.* strongly, 1318; *adj.* stiff, 2336

stigh *n.* path, 1405

stikkes *n. pl.* sticks, 126

stille, stil *adj.* motionless, 429, 3028

stilly *adv.* quietly, 1443

stir *v.* move, bring forward, 1008

stith *adj.* strong, bold, 2934

stode *v. pt.* stood, 520 **stont** *v.3 sing.* (**stondeth**) stands, 382

stoffe *n.* stuff, material, 1084

stol *n.* stool, 1262

stoppel *n.* bottle stopper, 724

store *n.* (*farm stock*) store, amount, 288, 604

stored *pp.* stored, kept, 2091

stound *n.* time, occasion, 94, 454, 1650

stour *n.* tumult, bad condition, 24

stowe *n.* place, clearing, 342, 1169

strad *v. pt.* strode, 294, 615

strangely, strangly *adv.* strongly, bitterly, 301, 990

straughte *v. pt.* stretched, 910, 1018, 1342

straunge *adj.* strange, 15, 348

straungely *adv.* in odd or peculiar fashion, 208

streight *adj.* straight, stretched out, narrow, 37

streit *adj.* straight, tall, 999; narrow, 846; *adv.* straightaway, forthwith, 2757

strengly *adv* strongly, vehemently, 1260

strewe *v. pt.* has scattered, strew, 1258

strike *v.* strike, stride, proceed, 1624 **strook** *v. pt.* struck, 1624b; proceeded, 1744

stryf *n.* strife, quarrelling, 1763

stykkes *n. pl.* sticks, 450

stynt *v.* stop, 694, 2378, 2698

sucre *n.* sugar, 2097

suffred *v. pt.* suffered, appeared at a disadvantage, 971

sujets *n. pl.* subjects, 2329

suked *v. pt.* sucked, 951

sundri *adj.* various, 267, 653

superfluitee *n.* excess, 394

superscripture *n.* (*what is written above*) title, address, 286

suppos *v.* supposing, 1477

supresed *v. pt.* suppressed, 2757

swalwed *v. pt.* swallowed, 892

swam *v. pt.* swam, 267

swanes *n. pl.* swans, 1940

sweven *n.* dream, 3017

swike *v.* deceive, 2312

swynes *n. pl.* pigs, 897

swyre *n.* neck, 1092, 1945

syn *prep.* since, 376

sythen *adv.* since, thereafter, 1634

taedium vitae *n.* (*Latin*) weariness of life, 409

taille *n.* tally, total, 2669

tak kepe *v. phr.* take notice of, watch out for, 430

talle *adj.* sturdy, strong, 1826

Taprobon *n.* Taprobana: Ceylon (Sri Lanka): island opposite and farthest from England on *mappaemundi*, 97

targe *n.* shield, target 184, 814

tartes *n. pl.* tarts, 2585

taske *n.* task, 1077

teche *v.* teach, 490

telle *v.* tell, 1532; count, 1381, 2676

teme *v.* subdue, tame, 502c

tene[1] *n.* distress, 586

tene[2] *v.* trouble, hurt, 200

tercel *n.* falcon, 470, 523

teres *n. pl.* tears, 238, 268, 302, 390, 395

terily *adv.* tearfully, 1103

termes *n. pl.* expressions, 524

tery *adj.* made of tears, 678; tearful, 2250

texte *n.* text, writing, 46

than *adv.* then, 326

thee, the *pr.* thee, 196, 299

theeched *pp.* thatched, 1472

thee'ch *v. phr.* so thee'ch, so thee'k indeed (as I [hope to] prosper), 280, 1112

theme *n.* text, subject, 1284, 1650

thenche *v.* think, 39 **thenchestow** (thenchest + thou) *v.2 sing.* do you think? 1019

thimbel *n.* thimble, 573

thi, thin *adj* thy, thine, your, 593, 709

thin[1] *adj.* thin, weak, 1734

thin[2] *see* **thi**

thistel *n.* thistle, 919

tho *adv.* then, 468, 559

thondered *v. pt.* thundered, 1932

thoru *prep.* through, 2544

thrawe *v.* throw, 2397

threst *v.* thrust, 915

thridde *n.* third, 1545 (*3rd May is mentioned several times in Chaucer's poems*)

thries *adv.* thrice, 1658

thrille *v.* pierce, 3056

thrive *v.* succeed, 1785

throly *adv.* strongly, boldly, 2426j

throng[1] *n.* throng, press, 1830

throng[2] *v. pt.* pressed, thrust, 544, 2426j

throstil *n.* thrush, 651

tidily *adv.* neatly, comfortably, 1670

tidy *adj.* of good condition or appearance, neat, 697, 715

timorously *adv.* nervously, 315

tinclen *v.* tinkle, 3067

to *adv.* too, 150, 370

togideres, togider *adv.* together, 482, 622, 836

tolde *pp.* told, 1000; *v. pt.* counted, 2329

toles *n. pl.* tools, instruments, 1288

tombeled *v. pt.* tumbled, 922

tonel *n.* tunnel; a tubular net for snaring birds, 37

tonge *n.* tongue, 630

toos *n. pl.* toes, 1921, 2425 (*also* **tos**)

tord *n.* turd, 443

torn *v.* turn, 1299 **torned** *v. pt.* 133 **tornyng** *pres. part.* 887

tos *n. pl.* toes, 286, 947

toti *adj.* giddy, unsteady, 1887

tough *adj.* tough, difficult **made hit tough** *v. phr.* took umbrage, 528, 1685

toun *n.* town, 3070 **out of toun** *adv.* away, 2018

trampeling *verbal n.* trampling, being trampled, 920

tre, treo *n.* tree, 1385, 2546d

trébuchet *n.* (*French*) artillery catapult, 273

trenche *n.* trench, pit, 40

trenchur *n.* carving knife; board or hunk of bread on which food was placed, 1553

trewe *adv.* truly, accurately, 542; *adj.* genuine, 2262

triacle *n.* treacle, medicine (*especially as an antidote to poison*), 1675

trompe *n.* trumpet, 2583 (*also* **trumpe**)

trone *n.* throne, 2577

trotters *n. pl.* boar's feet, 1026t; Mock Turtle's feet, 2421

troue, trow *v.* believe, trust, 428, 2452

trublen *v.* trouble, disturb, 2165

trumpe *n.* trumpet, 2650 **trumpes** *n. posses.*, 2642

tun *n.* barrel, 303

tung *n.* tongue, 928
twayn *n.* two, 836
twelfte *num. adj.* twelfth, 2361
tweye *n.* two, 1280
twinkelinge *n.* twinkling, moment, 1608
twyys *adv.* twice, 3
tyde *n.* time, 57, 1212
tye *v.* tie, 277
tyme *n.* time, opportunity, 627
tyrtull *n.* turtle-dove, 2546d
tyte *adv.* quickly, 289, 708
tyter *adv.* more quickly, 2066
ugsome *adj.* hideous, 2600
uncnawen *pp.* unknown, unheard of, 2531
uncrulled *v. pt.* uncurled, 1951
uncurteisly *adv.* rudely, discourteously, 1225
undertake *v.* undertake, employ, 523
undertoke *v. pt.* undertook, absorbed, understood, 2056
undo *v.* dissect, cut up (*as in hunting*), 2809
unesi *adj.* uncomfortable, 2597
unesid *pp.* uneasily, anxiously, 2686
unfrendli *adj.* unfriendly, 1005
unhap *n.* misfortune, 375
unhapi *adj.* wretched, unfortunate, 1896
unknowe *pp.* unknown, 415
unlustily *adv.* idly, slothfully, 1444
unlyc *adj.* unlike, different from, 322
unnaturel *adj.* against nature, 16
unnethe *adv.* scarcely, with difficulty, 1322, 1343
unredi *adj.* unready, incomplete, 2629
unriht *adj. and n.* unfair, injustice, 1802
untye *v.* untie, 613
unware *adj.* unaware, 1528
upbrayd, upbreyde *v. pt.* bristled up, 437, 611
up-so-doun *adv.* upside down, 92
us *n.* use, 167, 175
used *v. pt.* got used to, 1163
utred *v. pt.* uttered, 1928
vanesched *pp.* disappeared, 680 vanissht *v. pt.*, 1446
vekke *n.* witch, 772
veneisun *n.* venison, 2564k
veraili *adv.* actually, 23

verdit *n.* verdict, 2645
verie *adj.* true, exact, 3038
verily *adv.* truly, 2278
verray *adv.* truly, 1043
verso *n.* back (*of a page*), 2909
vinegre *n.* vinegar, 2096
vir *n.* (*Latin*) man, 2944c
voys *n.* (tone of) voice, 348, 518
wacchyng *pres. part.* watching, 1972
waik *adj.* weak
wain *n.* wagon, 876
wal *n.* wall, 560
waltrot *n.* nonsense, 289, 1106
wand *n.* (walking)stick, 554
wandryng *pres.part.* wandering, 3039
want *n.* lack, 502d
war *adj.* wary, aware of, 840
warde *v.* guard, 2582
wares *n. pl.* wares, merchandise, 2564n
warily *adv.* cautiously, 255
warloker *adv.* more cautiously, 34
wasschyng *verbal n.* wasshing, 2299
wastel bredes *n. pl.* fine white bread, 205
wayten *v.* wait, 174
weder *n.* weather
wedered *pp.* withered
weilaway! *interj.* alas!, 374
welle *n.* well, 41 welles *n. posses.* of the well, 48
wel *adv.* very, 83
welde *v.* wield, carry, 1156
welken, welkne *n.* sky, 274, 1122
wend *v.* go, 732, 2572; *pp.,* gone, 72
wene *v.* think, 322, 2099
wentestow *v. pt.* (wentest + thou) did you go?, 1085
wepe *v.* weep, 2256 wepte *v. pt.* wept, 270
werbled *v. pt.* warbled, sang, 2546f
werche *v.* work, 1148
weri *adj.* weary, 231; werieth *v.3 sing.* tires, wearies, 1651
werkand *pres. part.* (*Northern*) working, 807
wers *adj.* worse, 1721
wertow *v.* (wert + thou) if you were, 1222
weryyng *pres.part.* wearisome, 1037
west *n.* waist, 2134

wete *adj.* wet, 567

wha *pr.(Northern)* who, 812

whal *n.* whale, walrus, 400, 1341

what swa *adv.* what so (ever), at all, 2864

whelp *n.* puppy, dog, 316

wher[1] *conj.* whether, 10, 1840

wher[2] *conj.* where, 366

wherof *rel. pr.* of which, 412

wherunder *rel.pr.* under which, 1095

while *n.* time, 740

whirleth *v.3 sing.* whirls, hurls, 273

whistlen *v.* whistle, 912

whit *n.* little bit, 517

whityng *n.* whiting (*fish of genus merlangus*), 2426a; finely powdered chalk used to whiten, 2467

whyssyne *n.* cushion, 1484, 1836

wicke *adj.* contemptible, wicked, 476

wight[1] *n.* person, 55, 178, 277, 358

wight[2] *n.* weight, 58, 839

win *v.* win, 502f; attain to, reach, 393, 794

winsum *adj.* winsome, attractive, 2546e

wintrys *n. posses.* winter's, 539

wise[1], wis *adj.* wise, 185, 557; sensible, 2710

wise[2] *n.* manner, 192, 549, 3033

wissche *v.* wish, 635, 735

wissen *v.* inform, 489

wiste *v. pt.* knew, 487, 508c

witen, wit *v.* know, 510, 1001

withoute[1] *adv.* outside, 1331, 2840

withoute[2] *prep.* without, excluding, 166

witti *adj.* clever, wise, 2931

wlaffyng *n.* stammering, 2343

wo *n.* woe, misery, 1634

wode[1] *n.* wood, clump of trees, 900 (*also* wood[1])

wode[2] *adj.* mad, 1245 (*also* wood[2])

woful *adj.* miserable, 474

wol *v.* will, want(s), 332, 451

wolde *v. pt.* wanted to, 296 wolde hit *v. phr.* if it would, 165

wolleward *adv.* haywire, wool-gathering (wool-wards), 1173

won[1] *n.* a deal ful won, gret won *adv.phr.* enormously, plentifully, 298, 2245

won[2] *pp.* won, 551

wondred *v. pt.* wondered, 392

wondyr *n.* wonder, amazement, 2178; *adv.* wonderfully, 2 Wondyr Lond *n.* Wonderland, 269, 3081

wondyrest *v.2 sing.* (you) wonder, 2133

wone *n.* custom, wont, 1047

woned *v. pt.* dwelt, 1670 wonen *v.* dwell, 1450

wont *v.* are accustomed, 381

wonted *adj.* customary, 280

wood[1] *n.* wood, 1119

wood[2] *adj.* mad, 1120, 2411 wood wrath *adj.* furiously angry, 1960

wook *v. pt.* awoke, 1743

woot, wot *v.* know, 380, 1037; *v. pt.* knew, 1110, 1438

wordles *adj.* wordless, silent, 557

wortes *n. pl.* roots, vegetables, 1801

worth *v.* become, 2944h

worthi *adj.* worthwhile, 1016

worthschiply, worthshiply *adv.* respectfully, 1806, 2869

wot *see* woot

wouke *n.* week, 2333 woukes *n. pl.*, 1116

wrang *adj.* wrong, 1802

wrat *v. pt.* wrote, 2611

wrathe *v.* exasperate, get angry, 629, 1010

wrecchedom *n.* misery, 477

wrecchednesse *n.* wretchedness, misery, 769

wrenches *n. pl.* tricks, 936

wrenne *n.* wren, 2546f

wrickede *v. pt.* writhed, wriggled, 2680

writhe *n.* wreath

wrought *pp.* acted, 34

wrythen *v.* twist, writhe, 1122 wrythed *v. pt.*, 1154

wulle *n.* wool, 311

wundrunge *n.* wonder, amazement, 2825

wurth *v. pt.* became, 362

wyde *adj.* broad, outlandish, 524

wynde *n.* wind, 2576

wyndow *n.* window, 746

wyrm *n.* worm, 514

yare *adv.* long ago, 1450

ybrought *pp.* brought, 166

ycumen *pp.* come [*past participle*], is ycumen *v.* has come, 348a ydoon *pp.* done, 2042

ye¹ *n.* eye, 276, 928

ye² *pr.* ye, you (*subject form, plural*), 500; ye, you (*polite plural used for singular*), 462, 525

ye³ *adv.* yea, yes indeed, 570 , 794

yeman *n.* yeoman, farmer, 453

yerde *n.* stick, discipline, 2516

yere, yer *n.* year, 283, 1565

yerne *adv.* eagerly, 2328

yes *n. pl.* eyes, 13, 238, 306

yet *adv.* still (*i.e.*, also now), 122, 367

yeyed *v. pt.* yelled, cried. 1631

yfalle *pp.* fallen, 469

yfel *adj.* evil at yfel *prep. phr.* in bad case, 2032

ygo *pp.* gone, 1336 ygoon, *pp.* 3081

yifte *n.* gift, 2168 yiftes *n. pl.* gifts, 285, 2170

yis *adv.* yes, 511

yisterday *n.* yesterday, 322, 2492

ylaft *pp.* left, 998

ymaginacioun *n.* imagination, 1679

ynow *adv.* enough, 494, 733

yonge *adj.* young, youthful, 328

Youle, Yule *n.* Yule, Christmas, 283, 1026r

ypotamus *n.* hippopotamus, 266, 400

yvel *adj.* evil, wicked, 426, 2982

ywrought *pp.* wrought, constructed, 762

Alice's Adventures in Wonderland, by Lewis Carroll 2008

Through the Looking-Glass and What Alice Found There
by Lewis Carroll 2009

A New Alice in the Old Wonderland
by Anna Matlack Richards, 2009

New Adventures of Alice, by John Rae, 2010

Alice Through the Needle's Eye, by Gilbert Adair, 2012

Wonderland Revisited and the Games Alice Played There
by Keith Sheppard, 2009

Alice's Adventures under Ground, by Lewis Carroll 2009

The Nursery "Alice", by Lewis Carroll 2010

The Hunting of the Snark, by Lewis Carroll 2010

The Haunting of the Snarkasbord, by Alison Tannenbaum,
Byron W. Sewell, Charlie Lovett, and August A. Imholtz, Jr, 2012

Snarkmaster, by Byron W. Sewell, 2012

Alice's Adventures in Wonderland,
Retold in words of one Syllable by Mrs J. C. Gorham, 2010

Alice's Adventures in Wonderland,
Printed in the Ewellic Alphabet, 2013

Alice's Adventures in Wonderland,
Printed in the Nyctographic Square Alphabet, 2011

Alice's Adventures in Wonderland,
Printed in the Shaw Alphabet, 2013

Alice's Adventures in Wonderland,
Printed in the Unifon Alphabet, 2013

Behind the Looking-Glass: Reflections on the Myth of
Lewis Carroll, by Sherry L. Ackerman, 2012

Clara in Blunderland, by Caroline Lewis, 2010

Lost in Blunderland: The further adventures of Clara
by Caroline Lewis, 2010

John Bull's Adventures in the Fiscal Wonderland
by Charles Geake, 2010

The Westminster Alice, by H. H. Munro (Saki), 2010

Alice in Blunderland: An Iridescent Dream
by John Kendrick Bangs, 2010

Rollo in Emblemland, by J. K. Bangs & C. R. Macauley, 2010

Gladys in Grammarland, by Audrey Mayhew Allen, 2010

Alice's Adventures in Pictureland,
by Florence Adèle Evans, 2011

Eileen's Adventures in Wordland, by Zillah K. Macdonald, 2010

Phyllis in Piskie-land, by J. Henry Harris, 2012

Alice in Beeland, by Lillian Elizabeth Roy, 2012

The Admiral's Caravan, by Charles Edward Carryl, 2010

Davy and the Goblin, by Charles Edward Carryl, 2010

Alix's Adventures in Wonderland:
Lewis Carroll's Nightmare, by Byron W. Sewell, 2011

Áloþk's Adventures in Goatland, by Byron W. Sewell, 2011

Alice's Bad Hair Day in Wonderland,
by Byron W. Sewell, 2012

The Carrollian Tales of Inspector Spectre
by Byron W. Sewell, 2011

Alice's Adventures in An Appalachian Wonderland
Alice in Appalachian English, 2012

Алесіны прыгоды ў Цудазем'і, *Alice* in Belarusian, 2013

Crystal's Adventures in A Cockney Wonderland
Alice in Cockney Rhyming Slang, 2014

Alys in Pow an Anethow, *Alice* in Cornish, 2009

Alices Hændelser i Vidunderlandet, *Alice* in Danish, 2014

La Aventuroj de Alicio en Mirlando,
Alice in Esperanto, by E. L. Kearney, 2009

La Aventuroj de Alico en Mirlando,
Alice in Esperanto, by Donald Broadribb, 2012

Trans la Spegulo kaj kion Alico trovis tie,
Looking-Glass in Esperanto, by Donald Broadribb, 2012

Les Aventures d'Alice au pays des merveilles
Alice in French, 2010

Alice's Abenteuer im Wunderland, *Alice* in German, 2010

Nā Hana Kupanaha a ʻĀleka ma ka ʻĀina Kamahaʻo,
Alice in Hawaiian, 2012

Ma Loko o ke Aniani Kū a me ka Mea i Loaʻa iā ʻĀleka ma
Laila, *Looking-Glass* in Hawaiian, 2012

Aliz kalandjai Csodaországban, *Alice* in Hungarian, 2013

Eachtraí Eilíse i dTír na nIontas, *Alice* in Irish, 2007

Lastall den Scáthán agus a bhFuair Eilís Ann Roimpi
Looking-Glass in Irish, 2009

Le Avventure di Alice nel Paese delle Meraviglie
Alice in Italian, 2010

L's Aventuthes d'Alice en Êmèrvil'lie, *Alice* in Jèrriais, 2012

L'Travèrs du Mitheux et chein qu'Alice y démuchit,
Looking-Glass in Jèrriais, 2012

Alicia in Terra Mirabili, *Alice* in Latin, 2011

La aventuras de Alisia en la pais de mervélias
Alice in Lingua Franca Nova, 2012

Alice ehr Eventüürn in't Wunnerland
Alice in Low German, 2010

Contoyrtyssyn Ealish ayns Çheer ny Yindyssyn
Alice in Manx, 2010

Dee Erläwnisse von Alice em Wundalaund
Alice in Mennonite Low German, 2012

The Aventures of Alys in Wondyr Lond
Alice in Middle English, 2013

L'Aventuros de Alis in Marvoland, *Alice* in Neo, 2013

Ailice's Anters in Ferlielann, *Alice* in North-East Scots, 2012

Die Lissel ehr Erlebnisse im Wunnerland,
Alice in Palantine German, 2013

Соня въ царствѣ дива: Sonja in a Kingdom of Wonder,
Alice in Russian, 2013

ʻO Tāfaoga a ʻĀlise i le Nuʻu o Mea Ofoofogia,
Alice in Samoan, 2013

Ailice's Àventurs in Wunnerland, *Alice* in Scots, 2011

Eachdraidh Ealasaid ann an Tìr nan Iongantas,
Alice in Scottish Gaelic, 2012

Alice's Adventirs in Wonderlaand, *Alice* in Shetland Scots, 2012

Alices Äventyr i Sagolandet, *Alice* in Swedish, 2010

Ailis's Anterins i the Laun o Ferlies,
Alice in Synthetic Scots, 2013

Alice's Carrànts in Wunnerlan, *Alice* in Ulster Scots, 2013

Der Alice ihre Obmteier im Wunderlaund
Alice in Viennese German, 2012

Ventürs jiela Lälid in Stunalän, *Alice* in Volapük, 2013

Lès-avirètes da Alice ô payis dès mèrvèyes,
Alice in Walloon, 2012

Anturiaethau Alys yng Ngwlad Hud, *Alice* in Welsh, 2010

CPSIA information can be obtained
at www.ICGtesting.com
Printed in the USA
BVHW030235081019
560479BV00001B/71/P